Tales from the 5th Street Gym

UNIVERSITY PRESS OF FLORIDA

Florida A&M University, Tallahassee
Florida Atlantic University, Boca Raton
Florida Gulf Coast University, Ft. Myers
Florida International University, Miami
Florida State University, Tallahassee
New College of Florida, Sarasota
University of Central Florida, Orlando
University of Florida, Gainesville
University of North Florida, Jacksonville
University of South Florida, Tampa
University of West Florida, Pensacola

1963

Tales from the 5TH ST. GYM

Ali, the Dundees, and Miami's Golden Age of Boxing

Ferdie Pacheco

With contributions by
Tom Archdeacon
Angelo Dundee
Suzanne Dundee Bonner
Enrique Encinosa
Howard Kleinberg
Ramiro Ortiz
Edwin Pope
Frankie Otero
Bob Sheridan
and Budd Schulberg

University Press of Florida
Gainesville · Tallahassee · Tampa · Boca Raton
Pensacola · Orlando · Miami · Jacksonville · Ft. Myers · Sarasota

15   14   13   12   11   10   6   5   4   3   2

Library of Congress Cataloging-in-Publication Data
Tales from the 5th Street Gym: Ali, the Dundees, and Miami's
golden age of boxing/Ferdie Pacheco; with contributions by Tom
Archdeacon . . . [et al.].
p. cm.
Includes bibliographical references.
ISBN 978-0-8130-3436-2 (alk. paper)
1. Boxing—Florida—Miami—History. 2. 5th Street Gym (Miami,
Fla.) I. Pacheco, Ferdie. II. Archdeacon, Tom.
GV1125.T35 2010
796.8309759'3819–dc22   2009037997

The University Press of Florida is the scholarly publishing agency
for the State University System of Florida, comprising Florida
A&M University, Florida Atlantic University, Florida Gulf Coast
University, Florida International University, Florida State Univer-
sity, New College of Florida, University of Central Florida, Univer-
sity of Florida, University of North Florida, University of South
Florida, and University of West Florida.

University Press of Florida
15 Northwest 15th Street
Gainesville, FL 32611–2079
http://www.upf.com

I respectfully dedicate this book to the public that makes up the wide audience for boxing in the world and to the participants, from promoters to managers to trainers to corner men to referees to judges and finally to the corps of boxers.

Contents

Acknowledgments

It is impossible to accurately list the hundreds of colleagues, friends, relatives, and acquaintances who contributed in some fashion to this book. I'll limit myself to the main contributors who are the entire body of work, the entire collection that makes up the table of contents, the inhabiters of the 5th Street Gym, and everyone in the world of boxing, worldwide. I owe them this book.

I start my small list of actual major contributors with my main one, my wife, Luisita, who spent many years typing my manuscripts, editing them, helping me to censor my mind and, when applicable, suggesting the addition of necessary extra material. To her goes the credit for the addition of the best chapter in the book, the one by Suzanne Dundee Bonner in a fine, heartfelt good-bye to her dad, Chris Dundee. If you don't cry when you read this masterpiece of writing, chances are you are dead.

There are excellent examples of the highest level of journalists who shared the wonders of the 5th Street Gym with me and inspired me. I give them thanks. The main one of all is the world-famous award-winning Budd Schulberg, who in addition to his time in the gym also travelled the world in the hilarious journey that Muhammad Ali took us on, as passengers on his Ali Train. On a daily basis, we shared years with Ed Pope, sports editor of the *Miami Herald*; with a piquant Old

South point of view, he brought the foibles of the 5th Street Gym under his amused gaze, lobbing off column after column of tongue-in-cheek ink exerted incisively with a distinct flavor of Mark Twain. He has become a close friend.

Another friend is Howard Kleinberg, who rose rung by rung up the employment ladder at the *Miami News* to be editor of the newspaper until it folded. He loved the 5th Street Gym, and when his star ascended and even as sports editor he had no time to write, he amassed a corps of sportswriters who fell upon the 5th Street Gym and devoured the beast. The best of these sportswriters was Tom Archdeacon, thumbnailed thusly by Kleinberg: "I'd send Archdeacon out to do a column. I wouldn't hear back for a week and then he'd show up with a novel."

Thrown in among the rough and rowdy journalists, boxers and their element, and the hundreds of fans who used him for information was a quiet, courtly, modest, self-effacing, ex–Coast Guardsman and immigration officer who showed up at the gym one afternoon. He parked himself on the ringside seats and began a lifetime of observing the life of boxing. He began gathering facts, newspaper magazines, and photos, until his house soon became crammed with boxing information. His name was Hank Kaplan, and it is my great sorrow to report that he did not live to see the publication of this book. He died without seeing the many pictures he gave me to use and owing me a chapter. He is one of the many old men who hung around the 5th Street Gym, simply because it was home and because boxers and promoters were their family. And they were all lovable. The best I can say for Hank Kaplan is that when he died he was credited with being *the* outstanding ring historian. And he was.

Thanks to my friends Angelo Dundee, Ramiro Ortiz, John Underwood, and Bob Sheridan for their contributions to this book. A heartfelt thanks to Enrique Encinosa for his wonderful chapters and for correcting the manuscript and giving us photographs from his collection. Many thanks to a great photographer, Jim Gestwicki, for without his photographs this book would not have looked the same, and to Ed Pierce for the use his great pictures. Also, thanks to Dwaine Simpson for his contribution of many photographs of the people who were part of the 5th Street Gym. For many years, he helped young amateur boxers and worked hard for them to become champions. His work has not gone unnoticed. He was with the Dundees for twenty years at the 5th Street Gym and fought for Chris thirty-five times as a preliminary fighter. Also, thanks to Steve Litzman at Photo Arts for helping take care of details with photographs.

Writers need fellow writers to read their work and criticize it and give their opinion, to praise or damn it but in some way discuss it. I must thank a source of criticism: his name is David Lawrence. He is an important man in Miami. He was the publisher and editor of the *Miami Herald* and, as such, was an influential voice in this community. I found him very genial, and for some reason he took a fancy to my writing. I started sending him my dream short stories and chapters from my latest books. I was shocked to be the recipient of the David Lawrence blitz: the great man receives your work, reads it, criticizes it, and puts it in the return mail. I've spent ten years sending this kind man my work. He has never failed to mail back his opinion. I've come to rely heavily on his opinion. I look forward to his reading this book, because it is his kind of book; it is a book about the people of Miami, about their trials and tribulations and sometimes victories.

I finish the acknowledgments at the point where I started, my wife, Luisita. We've now worked together for thirty-eight years. She came to me as a bright, fresh, young flamenco dancer with an inquisitive mind. She was open to learning anything and everything. She couldn't come into my world of medicine, and even boxing was a stretch, but her bright brain absorbed the world of letters, and her creative sense stretched to include the art world. Not only was she a huge help, but soon she started to paint as well. And she was good.

The world of letters was wide open to her. There was plenty of hard work to be done, as life raced past me. Publishers spoke on computers, and the new technology led to a process of submitting manuscripts that was beyond my talents. "Not me," I said. "I write with my Mont Blanc white ball fountain pen on legal stationery." That obviously was the end of my writing career before I'd gotten even two books published.

My wife stepped up to the plate. With index finger upraised, she said, "I can do that. Buy a computer. I can learn." And she did. We have now had sixteen books published, all the work done by her. So forgive a bit of husbandly bragging, but you wouldn't be reading this book if Luisita had not applied herself diligently to the hard work of typing, organizing, and getting the photos and editing this book.

Preface

The Wizard of Oz

Once upon a time, in the land of coconuts and orange blossoms, of stately royal palms, clear skies, sunlit beaches, high turf, and eternal summer, there existed a magic place on the corner of 5th Street and Washington Avenue. The 5th Street Gym was our earthly equivalent of the kingdom of Oz.

Like Oz, it was run by a wizard. His name was Chris Dundee, and he ran his place of continuous joy with the help of his brother, the Prince of Oz, whose name was Angelo, for no better reason than that he was an Italian from Philly. They had an army of aged dwarfs helping to run the place, and these were called the gray men. The gray men formed a college of opinion and knowledge and their self-perceived job was to offer an opinion on every occurrence that took place inside the palace. Every gray man had been sent to the Wizard, because he held an important position: Minister of the Bureau of Insignificant Persons.

Boxing people the world over sent their fighters to be trained in the 5th Street Gym. Every possible thing that could be taught about the grim profession of boxing was taught by the Wizard, because, as he so often said, "Who knows more about boxing than me?"

It lasted for more than three decades and produced a great number of world champions. Its worldwide fame was the consequence of having given birth and sustenance to Cassius Clay, who soon changed his name to Muhammad Ali—in time to wreck the gate for Chris, who aged two decades during the now legendary Clay-Liston title fight.

Still, Ali remains the shining accomplishment of Oz. We're all touched by his fame—though eventually he eclipsed even the fame of the Wizard of Oz, who was forced by the ruling bodies of boxing to turn over his title of Chief of the Bureau of Truly Insignificant People. This in turn gave rise to the Ali Circus of hangers-on, who, in turn, eclipsed the gray men.

Eventually, time caught up to the palace and the gray men disappeared. Even the Wizard of Oz, Chris, had a stroke and quietly expired.

So it was, then, on one bright afternoon in 2006 that the mayor of Miami Beach, David Demer, called survivors—Ali, Angelo, and me—to the corner of 5th Street and Washington Avenue to unveil a plaque. The building that housed the 5th Street Gym had been torn down to make room for a parking lot. Next to it on a building hung the plaque dedicated to Angelo Dundee.

Chris Dundee. Hank Kaplan Archive, Brooklyn College Library.

Left to right, foreground: Ali, Angelo, and Ferdie at the unveiling by Miami Beach mayor David Deme of the plaque for the 5th Street Gym. Luisita Sevilla Pacheco.

One omission was so glaring that I had to bring it up. Nowhere on the plaque or in the remarks by the dignitaries was there mention of the Wizard of Oz himself, Chris Dundee. Of course I rectified that in my remarks, but I went home steaming. Chris, the Wizard, was not yet cold in his grave and he had already vanished from public sight!

That in a nutshell is the reason for this book. Read it and enjoy the wonderful place that was the 5th Street Gym.

The 5th Street Gym

Boxing cannot exist in a city without a good gym to train and prepare the boxers in and from which the promoter can book his fighters all over the world.

In Miami, for over thirty years, such a gym was the 5th Street Gym, the jewel in the crown of fight gyms. Ring historians admired it: the venerable Hank Kaplan, for example, once said, "During the golden era of boxing, from the forties to the eighties, there were four gyms close in importance to the 5th Street Gym. They were Gleason's and Stillman's Gyms in New York and the Main Street Gym in L.A. and Furkie's Gym behind a pool parlor in the East New York Brownsville section in Brooklyn. But at the head of the short list there was always, number one, the 5th Street Gym."

"The name fighters, the biggest names who paraded through there were Muhammad Ali, the biggest attraction of all, Luis Manuel Rodriguez, Carmen Basilio, Emile Griffith, Joe Louis, Archie Moore, Sugar Ray Robinson, Sonny Liston, Joey Maxim, Jimmy Ellis, Roberto Duran, Sugar Ramos, Ralph Dupas, Willie Pep, and Willie Pastrano. All world champions in their divisions," said Angelo Dundee, the world's most famous corner man, who trained eight of these champs who trained at the 5th Street Gym.

During the golden age, all of the contenders who aspired to the championship trained there—and that is a formidable list, a Who's

Newlyweds Chris and Gerry Dundee. Hank Kaplan Archive, Brooklyn College Library.

Who of boxing in that thirty-year period. In short, the 5th Street Gym was at the epicenter of boxing in America and so, by extension, the world. It was truly the mecca of boxing.

The 5th Street Gym was born out of necessity by the expert promoter Chris Dundee, who began promoting fights in Miami Beach and recognized a rich venue for weekly fights. He had come up the hard way from Philly club fights to Madison Square Garden under the watchful eye of mob boss Frankie Carbo, who controlled boxing in the 1940s. Chris then shifted to Norfolk, Virginia, as the U.S. Navy beckoned during wartime. He made a small fortune there and developed Midget Wolghast and Ken Overlin as world champions and a large stable of promising contenders that kept Chris busy managing fighters and promoting fights in the wartime navy town.

Chris made his first trip to Miami in 1938, when he brought Ken Overlin to fight Ben Brown in the jai alai fronton. Twelve years later, Chris remembered the lucrative date and the absence of regular boxing in the balmy vacation capital of the country, Miami Beach. Soon after, he moved—lock, stock, and barrel—and began thirty years of successful boxing promotions there. His 1957 promotion of the lightweight "World's Championship" Wallace "Bud" Smith–Joe Brown fight gave him a national name.

Chris *(left)* in the 1930s with a boxer. Hank Kaplan Archive, Brooklyn College Library.

Left to right, foreground: Chris Dundee with Kid Gavilan and Trevor Berbick at the 5th Street Gym. Jim Gestwicki.

When he had established a weekly boxing promotion, he felt he needed a gym to provide his promotion with a continuing supply of fresh boxing faces. So in 1950, Chris found an empty space above Howie's Bar and Liquor Store, the Thrifty Market, and a large corner drugstore in front of which was a big newsstand that featured out-of-town newspapers, especially all the papers from New York.

It was located at 501 Washington Avenue, at the corner of 5th Street and Washington Avenue. By 1950, South Beach was beginning its long spiral downward into decadence and decay. The money went north as Miami Beach built the Fontainebleau, Eden Roc, Diplomat, and Americana hotels and the era of gigantic condos pushed South Beach into the shadows.

The 5th Street Gym became the tourist attraction of South Beach. As shabby and unkempt as its surrounding real estate, the 5th Street Gym somehow "belonged." Visitors expected to visit a grubby gym,

1963

Cassius Clay in front of the 5th Street Gym talking to a fan. Ed Pierce/*Miami News*.

Boxers working out in the 5th Street Gym. Jim Gestwicki.

with a squeaky staircase, rotting floors, peeling paint, and leaky show-ers. The 5th Street Gym looked like a movie set and for good reason, since it was used in several movies. The ring was on the left side of the gym with chairs around one side so tourists could watch Ali train. The place was surrounded by windows: one in particular with "5th St Gym" painted on it. There was a freestanding mirror placed against the wall where fighters could train by looking at their moves. At the far end of the gym was a hook for a punching bag for the fighters to punch for practice. And in-between, all the fighters shadowboxed, jumped rope, and trained hard by hitting the bag that the trainers held. There was movement in the gym. In the back was a small room where the fighters got their massages from the great trainers such as Luis Sarria.

The 5th Street Gym probably reached its zenith with the first Cassius Clay–Sonny Liston bout on February 25, 1964. The bout was fraught with danger and political upheaval as Cassius decided to announce to the world that he had converted to the Muslim faith. There were more than eight hundred reporters present, and they were treated to the biggest sports upset of the century. Cassius Clay TKO'd the heavy favorite, Sonny Liston, in seven rounds!

The dateline their shocking story carried was "Miami Beach," and most stories during the six-week training period carried the dateline "5th Street Gym." The world recognized the name! The 5th Street Gym, which came to be recognized as Boxing in America, had become internationally known.

Sonny Liston training. Ed Pierce/*Miami News*.

Ali hitting heavy bag. Luisita Sevilla Pacheco.

The gym flourished while Ali's career was perking along. Every time Ali came down to train, the place filled up with fans, and Chris would promote great fights.

But as Ali's flame flickered out in the late 1980s, so did the 5th Street Gym. Not even Angelo's vast stable of fighters were enough to make it financially viable. Time savaged its already shaky foundations, and the building began to disintegrate.

All good things run their course, and certainly the 5th Street Gym would run its course when the king, Chris, grew old and retired, for without Chris, the 5th Street Gym would have no reason to exist. Angelo had become a world-renowned manager, trainer, and corner man, but he could not keep a gym filled with fighters.

Chris was surprised by a devious assault by a furniture manufacturer, Mel Zeigler, who decided one night that Chris should not be allowed to have exclusivity for the Miami Beach Auditorium. Anyone should be able to take a date and promote boxing!

Well, what qualifications did he bring to the promotion? Zeigler dug up an old retired promoter, Major Peoples, to put up a fancy front. They did promote one important fight: Bob Foster versus Vicente Rondon for the unification of the light heavyweight title. Foster won the crown, but Mel Zeigler lost his ass. He found that the streets of boxing were not paved with gold. Without Chris, boxing in Miami Beach shriveled and died. Without continuous boxing every Tuesday, it was not a financially healthy proposition.

It is regrettable to observe the inconstancy of the political animal and how quickly gold buys opinion and votes. Small minds cost the city its yearly rent and percentage, and that hurt. Chris held his ground and would not promote unless he had exclusivity. Boxing died, and the 5th Street Gym was no longer needed. Chris closed the place in time; that was a sad day.

A fan named Roosevelt Ivory took it over and tried to keep it open, but he didn't last. Boxing promoter Tuto Zabala likewise tried to keep it open, but he too succumbed. They put old champion Beau Jack in the gym to keep it open. Jack lived in the gym and took no money, but still, in time, the writing was on the wall.

Soon, with his life taken from him, Chris had a damaging stroke. He was taken to live out his years as a paralyzed man without the ability to communicate. Chris, the master salesman and promoter, could not speak for the ten years left to him. It was truly heartbreaking to visit him. I would go to see him with recorded videotapes of NBC fights, then wait as he patiently scrawled his observations. His mind was sharp, but his communication was poor. In the end, I was left with a monologue that Chris could not answer. I lasted about five years, and then I lost heart. I could not subject my heart to that ordeal.

I will never forgive the imposters and self-inflated windbags for bribing their way past small-time politicians to rob a brilliant mind of his life.

There was a movement to convert the 5th Street Gym into a Hall of Fame for boxers, and the community supported the idea but did not produce the necessary funds.

Finally, with all hopes to save the building exhausted, in March 1993 the interior was gutted and the building demolished. Those few who were part of the old building were in tears as the wrecking ball did its work.

I took my wife, Luisita, to witness the memorable demolition. Lunch was called, and a television crew grabbed me to do a final interview. As the host started, I saw out of the corner of my eye Luisita lifting one end of a training table while a worker lifted the other, skulking across the background of my sad interview. It was all I could do to keep from bursting out in laughter. The table is now part of my art studio, still stout, strong, and functional. I suppose that when I'm gone the old training table will be worth a lot of money, and it'll go to Luisita—she earned it.

I hope that by reading this slim collection of boxing stories you can imagine how much fun we had, what important work we did there, and what we meant to boxing in this country. Long live the spirit of the 5th Street Gym! Today, the structure has been knocked down, but its memory will always survive. In its place a large building now stands. Miami Beach mayor David Demer installed a plaque on the site where the gym once stood. It's nice, but wouldn't you know it, Chris Dundee's name is nowhere.

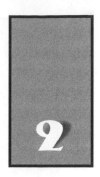

My Impression of the 5th Street Gym

Edwin Pope

Ed Pope is an award-winning *Miami Herald* sports editor and columnist. For four decades, he was the voice of sports in Florida. Ed Pope came to the *Miami Herald* as a diminutive temp from Georgia with a #2 Eagle pencil behind his ear and a green note pad in hand. His soft, appealing southern accent and charming, polite manner won over the sports room in no time. The little kid could write, and small though he was, he was tough in a pinch. His history is bright, replete with every award given to a man who writes sports. He is deadly accurate in reporting a news event, but he writes with an appealing sense of humor. You feel the South in his prose, a strong touch of Mark Twain. Pope is fun to read. So, skipping his vast curriculum vitae, I'll jump to the conclusion. I wanted one voice to summarize the 5th Street Gym, an expert who lived through its grand years and mourned its passing. There is only one Edwin Pope. There is none other.

My Impression of the 5th Street Gym

In the sleazy but nonetheless compelling chaos of Times Square in the 1930s, Chris Dundee was just beginning the boxing life that would make him the legend of the 5th Street Gym in Miami Beach. Chris was managing here and promoting there, just trying to put bread on the table.

His connections included Madcap Maxie Baer. Today, Baer's son is best known as the handsome yokel in TV's *Beverly Hillbillies*, but the original Max was heavyweight champion until his reluctance to apply himself to anything

Left to right: Ed Pope, Ferdie Pacheco, and Pauline Winick. Luisita Sevilla Pacheco.

Chris *(left)* in front of the deli with another boxing promoter and a fighter, 1930s. Hank Kaplan Archive, Brooklyn College Library.

very serious caught up with him—unless, that is, you consider a surfeit of willing women as very serious.

Chris was just getting ready to go to his office at the Hotel Edison when Baer called early one morning. "Get me a woman," Baer said to Chris.

The request, and others like it from Baer, always puzzled Chris Dundee: "One business I was never in was the woman business," he would say. But that morning he simply told Baer, "Don't call me at home. Call me at the office."

"I can't, Chris," Baer said.

"Why can't you, Maxie?"

"Because," said Baer, "I can't wait."

Chris hung up and probably spent the day grinning. He was the master of that, having the greatest grin in boxing or a lot of other places. The grin was the trademark of the little swashbuckler, who died at age ninety-one in 1998. That grin was part of what made satellites out of all the big names that whirled around him, including Muhammad Ali.

I agree with Ferdie Pacheco that Chris was the most fascinating of all boxing people—the most engaging person I have known in my seventy years in all sports, for that matter. And that includes his brother, Angelo, who was among the most able and amiable of men; the deceptively good-natured Rocky Marciano; the altogether singular Willie Pastrano, a man who would leave few worldly appetites unfulfilled; and a gross ton of other nonforgettables.

I have considered an incident—a vow of secrecy, really, that I took in Chris's office one of the first times I met him—and I have concluded that the statute of limitations has run out sufficiently for me to tell the story. You are begged only to recall a particular relationship between boxing and the media before far stricter sets of ethics were applied (at least on the media side), some years ago.

Chris used his old office in the Miami Beach Auditorium as a fulcrum to vault to the 5th Street Gym and back and all over the world. Maybe he didn't need an office. The inside left pocket of a sports jacket would do as well. He was forever yanking out a wad of papers and bills held together by an omnipresent rubber band. He must have bought them wholesale.

Left to right: Chris in his office with Nat Fleisher (owner and editor of *Ring* magazine) and Luis Godoy from Havana, Cuba. Chris Dundee Collection.

Whatever, he was standing in his office (he almost never sat down) that day in 1956, going on about how much he loved South Florida—more than his old environs in Philadelphia and New York. I asked him exactly why he felt this way.

"I'll tell you why!" It was Angelo interrupting. Angelo was just a pup then. He reached into a file cabinet and brought out a tiny book and opened it for me. It showed dates and the names of arenas where Chris had promoted fights before coming to Miami Beach. It also showed numbers—not dollar marks, just numbers—and then a couple of initials.

"What's this?" I asked (Gullible's Travels).

"Chris's payoff list," Angelo said. He elaborated on the numbers, which ranged from about $30 to $300. He also explained the initials. They stood for names of people who were in positions to enhance Chris's crowds. Some were sports writers, and some were gossip columnists.

Chris standing in the phone booth, with Moe Fleischer *(left)* and Marzo Fernandez *(right)*. Nat Fleisher, Ferdie Pacheco Collection.

"And that's why Chris likes it down here," Angelo said. "He doesn't have to pay off anybody." He paused. "Well . . ." Angelo named one notorious figure who both broadcast fights and managed fighters. "Except for him," Angelo said.

You wouldn't recognize most of the names.

But they were important back in the 1940s, before Chris and Angelo brought their brother act to the beach. Anyway, that was my introduction to Chris Dundee and, by extension, to the 5th Street Gym and its celebrated two flights of creaky stairs and the matchless cast of stars, loonies, and hustlers there.

It was another world.

And Chris created it and ran it.

He rented the space over a drugstore for the gym. He charged fighters small fees for lockers and showers. It mustn't have been much of a nut for the fighters. He didn't hear anybody who couldn't afford the tariff up there.

A huge bunch of worldwide celebrities went up those stairs, from Ali and Budd Schulberg to Red Smith and Howard Cosell to a laundry list of champions. Plenty of them made the vertical trip with killing hangovers. They felt like they were climbing Pike's Peak. I know. But it was always worth the climb, for anyone with even the most distant relationship with boxing.

The first guy you saw was Chris, right out of Schulberg's classic *The Harder They Fall*. He was a promoter/manager of screen and stage, except he never wore the turned-down fedora. Never, either, to my knowledge, did he smoke cigars.

He spent almost a century on the hustle. He started out as what they called a candy butcher—peddling Baby Ruth's (not, as most still mistakenly call them, "Babe Ruth's"). He was just ten years old when he plied that original trade on the trains from Philly to New York. You could do it back then.

Somewhere along the line, his last name, his square handle of Mirena, got changed to Dundee. "Nobody would give an Italian a break in boxing," Chris said. "So we thought we'd make ourselves sound like Irish."

A certain irony ran through that switch, because some not-at-all-Irish bent noses named Frankie Carbo and Blinky Palermo controlled the biggest chunk of boxing from just before midcentury. Somehow Chris made it work without the mob grinding him down. Both Chris and Angelo were brushed at birth with coatings of sheer functionality that hardly ever let them down.

I bring it up because this sense of survival seemed to be the heartbeat of the 5th Street Gym. The regulars included Mumblin' Sam Sobel, a onetime manager who was then without visible means of support, and Ben "Evil Eye" Finkle, Sobel's constant partner. Evil Eye claimed to have invented the double whammy, which is supposed to work as a hex and by which certain boxing people set some store. Finkle further (and often) claimed that "L'il Abner" artist Al Capp had stolen the double whammy. Capp probably did, but it would be hard to imagine Finkle standing up in court against a man of Capp's affluence, plagiarist or not.

So Chris's entire coterie, from Mumblin' Sam all the way up to Budd Schulberg and Howard Cosell accepted crazy as the norm. They were not violent people, but they lived on a special planet that consisted mostly of people doing violent things to each other.

One day Chris telephoned and said he had a "terrific" column for me. The subject turned out to be an ex-champion doing time in the Dade County stockade for extremely nefarious acts. Chris told me the name and said, "I'll take you up there Sunday." He added, "There is only one condition."

"What's that, Chris?"

"You can't write nothing bad about this guy," he said. I told Chris he must be kidding; the guy was definitely without honor—the highest praise Chris could confer upon anyone was "honorable." Anyway, I couldn't possibly do a column without mentioning why the fighter was locked up.

"Then I can't take you out there," Chris said. "He's the only guy in the world I ever been afraid of. He might kill me."

I demurred. That was that.

It was all part of the code that governed the lives of the 5th Street

Sugar Ray Leonard *(left)* and Roberto Duran *(right)*. Luisita Sevilla Pacheco.

Gym's denizens, from very low to very high. They accepted that everyone had to make a living and sometimes the ways of doing that were less than completely honorable. For example, stealing wasn't completely dishonorable, especially if you did it with a certain panache, and then it was expected that people could steal from you, too.

Such a world! If I hadn't been so hung up on football (which had its own kind of cheating, only far more hypocritical) and if boxing hadn't eventually plunged into its illegible jumble of alphabetized "champions," I sometimes wished I had tried to take up writing about boxing exclusively. Like race drivers and horse-racing people, everybody in boxing would *talk* to you.

Once for instance, only seconds after Roberto Duran's shocking "No mas!" loss to Sugar Ray Leonard in New Orleans, I rushed to Freddie Brown, one of Duran's corner men, and begged him to tell me what happened. "He just fucking quit," Brown said. "That's it. Just fucking quit."

Imagine getting such an audience with a central figure in a Super Bowl or World Series. But that was the way of the 5th Street Gym genre, with the exception of an occasional misanthrope such as Sonny Liston.

One of the few printable replies from Liston came after he dispatched the unfailingly upbeat Mike DeJohn. In their meeting in the Miami Beach Auditorium, DeJohn put a few bumps on Liston before Sonny started to work. Afterward, Liston said out of the side of his mouth, a style he had learned in prison for beating up guys long before DeJohn came along, "He made me bleed, so I decided to show him some of his own blood."

As a coincidence, both died in Las Vegas: Liston under strange circumstances and DeJohn of natural causes after he worked as a bartender and a card dealer. Quite a few other ex-boxers took to tending bar, which was a genteel trade contrasted with their previous line of work. One of these old fighters uttered what I held to be a rather memorable line after his bar's owner torched a place for insurance purposes. "It was a successful fire," the fighter said.

As for why I continued to call Clay, "Clay," I had good reason. My reasoning went like this. At the time of the first and second Liston fights,

Sonny Liston. Ted Press.

he was still called "Clay" about half the time and "Ali" the other half. Some of the time, thinking it was funny, I called him "formerly Cassius Clay." It enraged a lot of people. I thought the sect of his followers was dangerous, and I thought he was disloyal. I found him electrifying in the ring and amusing out of it, but you had to be a little nutty yourself to take seriously that stuff about "the big mother ship gonna shoot down bolts at the whites." And all the way from Miami to Massachusetts, for the schedules of the Liston fight, he bombarded me with jokes with the "n-word." So I couldn't get quite as hysterically dedicated to him as some were. I considered him a consummate clown with great timing, combining magnificent athleticism with terrific courage.

Cassius Clay walking up the stairs of the 5th Street Gym. Luisita Sevilla Pacheco.

3

My Memories of the 5th Street Gym

Angelo Dundee

My friend Ferdie asked me to write a little something about the 5th Street Gym. It was my home away from home. I earned my college degree at the 5th Street Gym. My children, Jimmy and Terry, would spend weekends there. Naturally, they suffered from my driving them from North Miami to 5th Street and Washington Avenue. By the way, my name is Angelo Dundee. I'm the kid brother of Chris Dundee.

During our long relationship, we never had an argument. Both being hard of hearing helped. I pride myself on naming the gym. I didn't let a guy from Boston who trained in the gym during the winter months pay dues. He told me that he was a painter and asked me if he could do some work around the gym. I told him to paint the windows and put the name "The 5th Street Gym" on one window. Since we never cleaned the windows, it also hid the smudges and the dirt. The flooring in the gym was all wood. Termites had a picnic there—it was old wood. The floor was getting thin and eaten away, so I replaced it with two-inch plywood and nailed it into the wood so it looked like a checkered board. Everybody enjoyed the posters of the fights on the wall. They didn't know that the posters were hiding the holes in it.

The 5th Street Gym was where I received my college degree in the art of training fighters. My professors from NYC read like a Who's Who in the profession: Chickie Ferrara, Charlie Goldman, Freddie Brown,

Chris *(left)*, Angelo *(right)*, and Ali (photo used as a Christmas card). Hank Kaplan Archive, Brooklyn College Library.

Jimmy August, Ray Arcel. I was their pupil. Working their corners as a bucket boy, I watched them train fighters daily at Stillman's Gym in New York City. All of them had their own technique of training. They were all great people. They were nice enough to teach me. Chickie taught me the art of wrapping the fighters' hands and tying their shoes, et cetera, et cetera, from the ground up. The luxury of my profession is that you never meet the same talent twice. They are all different. My brother Chris was a great teacher; from him I learned the art of the match makers, promoters, and newspapermen. He was a genius.

Chris Dundee (right) talking to Sean Connery. Hank Kaplan Archive, Brooklyn College Library.

Angelo Dundee *(right)* and Ernest Borgnine. Ferdie Pacheco Collection.

The 5th Street Gym brought superstars from all fields of endeavor. A day didn't go by that there wasn't a happening—never a dull moment. Having two or three world champs training there was a common occurrence. I enjoyed every minute. There will never be another 5th Street Gym.

Angelo and I

Ferdie Pacheco

When I asked Angelo to write a full chapter on what his life in the 5th Street Gym meant to him—how it impacted on his family life, on his boxing life, and on his life in general—I felt bad to ask. I've been very close to Angelo through our 5th Street Gym days, from the early 1960s to the present day. You have to understand the sterling character of

Angelo Dundee. But to ask him to open his heart and write about himself is downright unfair. It's not in his character.

Angelo, you see is the essence of self-effacement. He is shy. He is modest. He will not blow his own horn. Growing up in boxing he always had a star attraction to defer to: his brother Chris, a gigantic figure in the sport. Angelo came to work and worked like a slave. He never questioned his orders, he just performed. Eventually, Chris had Angelo plant each of these budding flowers and had him nourish them in the fertile field of the 5th Street Gym. They grew, flourished, and became world champions. The list is filled with illustrious champs: Willie Pastrano, Ralph Dupas, Luis Manuel Rodriguez, Mantequilla Napoles, Ultiminio Ramos. All were in that first wave of champions that washed over the 5th Street Gym. All were exceptional fighters, and all had one thing in common: Angelo Dundee.

Angelo lavished individual attention on each boxer. And when you got Angelo you got his boxing knowledge, his training knowledge, and the assured knowledge that you had the world's greatest corner man in your corner. If that wasn't enough, unspoken and unwritten about was the fact that Angelo brought with him his invisible team, for a boxing brain, the best in promotion and managing a boxer, his brother Chris Dundee hovered just over the horizon, invisible but always there, giving advice, counsel, and instruction. Angelo was the best boxing manager of his day because he had the best manager of managers in his ear.

In the gym, he had harvested a jewel of a trainer and conditioner in Luis Sarria, a quiet, dignified tower of strength and knowledge. Sarria came with Luis Manuel Rodriguez, who won as many fights by "out-conditioning" an opponent as by knocking him out with a fist. Angelo, with open arms, greeted Sarria as an equal, and Angelo, with his generous heart, recognized a master of conditioning.

Sarria began to help all of the Cuban boxers. And finally, to put our championship corner together, I joined their team as a boxing physician, taking care of all the boxer's needs and those of his family as well, all for no recompense. I didn't want to be paid, so I had a free and independent voice when tough choices had to be made. Angelo, free from the paranoia of old-time boxing trainers, correctly did not see me as a threat to him. I just wanted to help Angelo, to be an adjunct to a perfect corner. I wanted the world to recognize that Angelo Dundee was the greatest corner man in boxing.

The essence of our corner was this: Sarria took care of conditioning and corner massaging, etc., during the fight and kept quiet. I was there to help Angelo but was really useless unless there was an injury, and then I became vital. My other contribution was *to shut up.*

So, you see, only one voice was heard in the corner. If I spoke, it was to repeat what Angelo had just said. The fighter heard one voice, followed one order, and fought one fight: Angelo Dundee's fight.

Did you ever read any of this in the fight magazines of that day? No, not a word. Why? you might ask. The answer is that both Sarria and I were sworn to help Angelo, to protect him and to keep his life quiet. Angelo is a blessing in disguise. He neither sought nor accepted easy publicity. He was always available, and his amiable personality made an interview fun, but Angelo did not give up big meatballs of publicity. What he gave you, you already had. But he was so sweet, so accessible, so anxious to help that when you left him you were happy that you had gotten to spend quality time with him, but did he give you anything new? Did you learn anything new about his fighter or how he was going to fight the fight? What did you have to write about? Nothing. Nada. Puffs of air.

No, Angelo was naturally humble. He didn't give you a detailed game plan, because the truth is, in that genius head of his, he didn't have one. That part he could not share with you, because it was yet to be written. That part happened in Angelo's head after round one, and after round two, and as the fight progressed. That's why he was so good with Ali: they both made it up as they went along. The rope-a-dope was born in round one when Ali found he could lean on the loose ropes away from George Foreman's looping ponderous but ineffective hooks. Round two was different! And so, in each fight, Angelo read Ali's mind. Ali was a genius, but so was Angelo. He read Ali like a book, and his instructions in the corner mirrored exactly what Ali was thinking. Those two brains were unbeatable.

And so the 5th Street Gym exploded. The entire world of boxing writers descended upon the gym. Did we change? No, Ali was the same—funny, irreverent, predicting, and poetry spouting—while all the time, in between the jive, there was the silent African prince, Sarria, whose eyes never left Ali. With a flick of his hands or an eye signal, he could get Ali to shut down the showbiz and get back to work. Ali was shucking and jiving, but he was putting in serious training. Angelo supervised the training. He got what he wanted: an Ali in the best possible shape. I went along as an insurance policy to deal with small medical annoyances, such as the flu, upset stomachs, muscle pulls, and so forth.

I took care of problems with a minimum of distance, and the world outside the 5th Street Gym never knew. Who was Dr. Pacheco? As the squinty-eyed Muslim muscle men asked, "What do he do?"

Ali said, "Never mind. He belongs with me, Angelo, and Sarria. Leave him be."

I have only one Angelo story to tell, and I don't think it's ever been told in the detail it deserves. This is the story of Jimmy Ellis and his rise to the heavyweight championship. If I had to pick an example of Angelo's greatness, both professional and personal, it would not be of Ali. Ali's story belongs exclusively to Ali. He is a giant. All of us lived in his shadow. Ali didn't need us. Without us, there still would have been an Ali.

The real testament of Angelo's greatness, in my eyes, was what he did with Jimmy Ellis. It only lasted three years, but what a masterpiece of managing, of building a shot middleweight into a heavyweight champion in three years of corner work, masterminding, and out-thinking Jerry Quarry and Floyd Patterson.

Angelo had his hands filled with the Cuban champions Florentino Fernandez, Douglas Vaillant, Gomeo Brenan, and, of course, the man who took up all of his time, Muhammad Ali.

But did he have time for a broken-down, hungry young guy with a starving family of eight kids? Could Angie pay attention to Jimmy?

"O.K. Grab a broom. You're hired. Need an advance?" Angelo had radar when it came to a boxer being broke and needing money. Have you ever been stone broke? No food in the kitchen *broke*? Angelo knew that feeling. Angelo had heart.

Angelo and his fighters. *First row, left to right*: Douglas Vaillant, Florentino Fernandez, An-gelo Dundee, Luis Manuel Rodriguez, Muhammad Ali. *Second row, left to right*: Guillermo Dutschmann, Jose Legra, Willie Pastrano, Allan Harmon. *Third row, left to right*: Ernesto Corral, Hignio Ruiz, Luis Sarria, Ciro Garcia. Hank Kaplan Archive, Brooklyn College Library.

He advanced Jimmy the money, and as Angelo let go of his hand, Jimmy heard the words that made his heart sing: "Get in shape, Jimmy. We're getting you money fights. You won't be sweeping up too long from now on." Jimmy started pounding the bag.

Because he was from Louisville and a childhood friend of Ali, he had an entrance into our 5th Street Gym family. "Yeah, Jimmy be one of us. Let's help him." He was saved! We all pitched in to help Ellis.

The Jimmy Ellis Championship

Jimmy Ellis was at the end of his rope. His middleweight career had fizzled. He was going nowhere but down. He was too good to fight up-and-coming contenders but not good enough for a title match. He was in the limbo of good fighters on the way out, and he didn't have a manager to protect him, to get him good matches, to look out for him.

His personal life was a train wreck. Jimmy was a good, moral man. He had married his childhood sweetheart and rapidly produced eight children. As might be surmised, they were broke and starving. Jimmy was in a tight place. He was in his early thirties, with very little time left and no prospects for a future.

Jimmy had heard of Angelo and his stable of fighters, and the 5th Street Gym, and Chris, the Godfather, who watched over his fighters and protected them against the bad guys. Angelo, of course, opened his heart and his arms to this good-looking kid.

"I'll do any kind of job. I'll wash out the shower stalls, pick up the equipment, and sweep and mop the floors. Please, Mr. Dundee, I need a *job*." said Jimmy.

In no time he was a favorite of the gym. He was the janitor, no doubt about that, and he did a great job. In the first week, Angelo put Jimmy in to train. If someone needed a sparring partner, Jimmy was ready. From welterweights like Luis Rodriguez to light heavyweights like Willie Pastrano, Jimmy would give them a good sparring session. Willie, a stranger to pain, came off a good four rounds with Jimmy and said, "Angie, Jimmy punches like a heavyweight."

"I know. I know," said Angie, smiling.

"When you going to turn him loose?"

"Soon, Willie, soon." And Angie was off with his interior thoughts. Angie had a plan. Only he knew it. I certainly didn't.

It was December, a bitter cold night in Gotham City. The Garden billboard loudly proclaimed

WORLD HEAVYWEIGHT TITLE FIGHT
MUHAMMAD ALI vs. ZORA FOLLEY

All tickets had been sold out days earlier, and scalpers were getting rich. It was a hot ticket!

The politics of the times had Ali in a precarious position. He had turned down being drafted into the army. Courts had ruled that he couldn't fight again. That was being appealed by Ali's attorneys. While they awaited the Supreme Court ruling, Ali could fight: therefore, the Folley fight.

Zora Folley had been a very good heavyweight and fought under the shadow of Sonny Liston, Floyd Patterson, Ingo Johansson, Eddie Machen, and a few lesser names. He was just too good to risk a title shot with. He waited impatiently. Finally, the Garden came up with a dream fight (for Zora); he could fight Muhammad Ali. Angie and Chris felt it was a safe fight. Ali could beat Zora in an interesting fight.

Then came the Dundee magic. Chris, wheeling and dealing, drops a bombshell on Teddy Brenner at Madison Square Garden. The Garden had the undefeated #1 light heavyweight contender, Johnny Persol. He scored wins over Amos Lincoln—a fringe heavyweight contender—and over former light heavyweight champ Harold Johnson. If Ali KO's Zora early, how about if Ali goes again, next month (that is, in January), against Persol? Ali versus Johnny Persol. The Garden boys began counting the money!

"Yes, but we got to showcase Persol in a real fight. You got anybody?"

"Why, yes. I got a washed-up middleweight contender, Jimmy Ellis. He put on weight and a few years and he'll give Persol a real fight for five or six rounds."

"Persol beats him easy?" says Teddy, eyeing Chris suspiciously. They never trusted each other at all: they were two sharks warily circling each other!

"Mortal cinch," says Chris, smiling like a fox who has cornered a prize sheep.

So it was that Angelo, who was 100 percent busy with Ali and Sarria (who went nowhere with another fighter when Ali fought), came to me and told me I was taking Ellis to New York to fight in Madison Square Garden. I would take Lou Gross to help in the corner. I was in heaven for two reasons: first, that Angelo would trust me with the new kid; and second, that Angie thought we had a decent chance to win. Angie gave me a word of advice.

"Persol starts slow. Jimmy is in top shape. Persol is a dog. If you jump him in the first round there's a decent chance you'll end the fight there. Go, take a shot!"

I never did come to a conclusion what went on there. Why was I, who had never been the head corner man, entrusted with Jimmy Ellis? They put Lou Gross to manage the corner. That means put the stool in and take it out, handle the spit bucket. He was a bitter old-timer who thought anyone under 65 was a "shoemaker" and made sarcastic asides all during the fight. I figured I could handle him. And I had a mojo working for me that not even Angie knew about.

I had adopted Jimmy Ellis. He stayed in my apartment and ate all of his meals with me. We went to football games with the 'Canes and the Dolphins, and in general, we were buddies. Me, the doctor from the 5th Street Gym with an office in Overtown, who was with Angelo, and him, the starving middleweight who was going to fight the #1 light heavyweight in the world, Johnny Persol. What a pair! What a night in store for us!

I worked on Jimmy's brain until he was ready to burst. I got him ready to burst out of the gate and jump on Persol.

"What if I get tired?" Jimmy asked.

"The guy that takes the beating is the one who gets tired—not the guy who gives the beating!"

We pushed through the crowd. A few people recognized me and yelled, "Hey, Doc, aincha woiking wid Ali?"

"Yeah, after he knocks out Persol," I would answer to a chorus of boos and catcalls.

Left to right: Sarria, Jimmy Ellis, Angelo, and Ferdie. Ferdie Pacheco Collection.

Clearly, Jimmy Ellis was the underdog. The New Yorkers hated us.

We got to a dank hole of a dressing room. It had steam pipes and electrical cables hanging all over the room. We had to crouch to stand erect. It was the pits.

"Doesn't look like they like us," said Jimmy.

"They're going to like us less when you knock out their guy," I said, maintaining a brave front. The strange thing here, looking back on it today, was that I was so sure he was going to win. After all, for the previous six years, every title fight I had been in that Angie's fighters had fought, they'd won. So, why not Ellis? He was ready and in great shape.

We'd gotten to the Garden too early. Lou Gross was inpatient. He didn't believe Ellis had a shot. To him, the dungeon was indicative of what the Garden thought of Jimmy's chances.

Lou Gross went out to watch the undercard fights. I stayed with Ellis, working with him hard, until he was hot and ready! I looked at my watch: thirty minutes to glove time. He could either sit here and freeze or get up and work up a sweat. I told him, "I want you hot and ready to fight."

"I'll get tired," said Jimmy, reasonably.

"Stop thinking negative. You need to break a sweat. Be hot, be ready. When Persol answers the bell, his body will be hot, hot, and your body is in round four. You'll kill him, Jimmy! And if you get him in trouble, don't hold back, let everything go."

We went out to the hostile crowd, with boos, whistles, yells, and catcalls. I kept Jimmy's robe on and towels over his head. With all that gear on, Ellis was way bigger than Persol. I saw Persol's eyes get bigger. "We got him," I said to Ellis, who saw the same look of fear that I did. Persol was thinking, "Damn, I'm fighting a heavyweight."

What awaited the poor Persol was (for us) a thing of beauty. Ellis dismantled Persol. He fell through the ropes, then the canvas, and then it was all over. Ellis in a KO!

Ellis and I hugged. At that moment, I knew how Angelo feels when one of his fighters wins! Now I knew.

To return to Angelo (since it is his chapter): Angie took Ellis over and got him in a heavyweight elimination tournament. Of course, we drew all the favorites; nobody gave Ellis a shot. He'd beaten a light heavyweight convincingly, yes, but not a heavyweight.

We were matched with Leotis Martin, the tournament favorite to win it all. Ellis gave a stunning performance and TKO'd Martin in nine following Angelo's game plan. It was an easy win.

Step two: Oscar Bonavena had just come from a life-and-death blockbuster fight against Joe Frazier. Frazier beat Bonavena, but no matter, Ellis was still the *big* underdog. Angelo said simply, "You can beat this bull. You can knock him out." Jimmy had him knocked out on the floor several times and easily beat the Argentinean, administering a heavy beating along the way.

Left to right: Howard Cosell, Ferdie, Jimmy Ellis, and Angelo. Lynn Pelham.

That left us with Jerry Quarry, and here is where Angelo earned his spurs as a genius!

"Box him. Jab. Jab, stick, and move. When he gets close, smother him in a clinch. We'll *stink* out the joint, and we'll be heavyweight champs of the world!"

And so it was Angelo's greatest moment.

Angelo Dundee: A Genius in the Corner

You know it's easy to say Angelo is a genius. They say anybody is a genius in the corner when you have Muhammad Ali doing the fighting or Luis Manuel Rodriguez or Willie Pastrano or Ralph Dupas or Mantequilla Napoles, or Ultiminio Ramos. But how does Angelo do with lesser fighters? Just as good. He takes a good fighter and makes him great. He takes a mediocre kid and makes him an acceptable opponent. He makes the kid better.

Angelo putting headgear on Willie Pastrano. Hank Kaplan Archive, Brooklyn College Library.

As I began to take care of the boxers of the 5th Street Gym for Chris, he began to repay me by giving me choice first-row seats. Every night I sat right behind the blue corner, which was Angelo's corner. Most of his fighters fought in the blue corner, and I started a running conversation with Angelo as he worked. He was very friendly and nice.

I really began to understand boxing and the importance of the corner men. They really were part of the action. They felt the punches. They were sad to lose and were elated to win. It was exhilarating for me to watch them in action.

Willie Pastrano was Angelo's most noteworthy fighter then. He was very good, but he was a playboy. The guy just wouldn't prepare properly. He could box like a dream, but he had no appetite for going toe to toe if he didn't have to. He didn't have a big punch to begin with, and his disposition was toward peacefulness, not hostility. He drove Angelo crazy.

One night he was scheduled to fight Jessie Bowdry, a tough, top-ranked fighter. If Pastrano won, he would move into position for a title shot.

Willie Pastrano doing roadwork with his dog. *New Orleans Picayune.*

As the fight began, I saw a different face on Angelo. He was tight, red faced, big eyes bulging. He danced around in the corner throwing punches in the air, yelling instructions that Pastrano would never hear.

By mid match, Angelo was hoarse. He was furious because Pastrano was running but not fighting and was losing, blowing his important opportunity.

By round six, Angelo started to turn green—I swear, it looked like the pallor that comes from coronary insufficiency. I thought he was going to have a heart attack. I tried to warn him, to calm him down. Angelo did not hear me; he had Jessie Bowdry to contend with, not his heart. People around me started to notice and yelled to him to calm down. Angelo was in a zone. Only the fighter mattered. "Wow! Now that is focus," I thought.

The fight ended. Somehow, Pastrano lost unanimously.

I started to work in the corners with Angelo, and I considered it a great privilege. I'm a quick learner. I could see I had a lot to learn, and Angelo was the best professor in the world.

Angelo made me feel welcome. I did not intrude. I was there to learn, not give my opinion. Angelo was a great cut man, so I would not presume to do the cuts. After the fight, when the cut is hot, I would immediately sew them up. In forty years of boxing, I never had a wound infection. Grudgingly, I was accepted by Angelo. I wouldn't get in his way. I would support anything he said. I was supportive in taking care of the out-of-the-ring family problems of the boxers and did not charge any of them. I took heat off of Angelo. And Chris, above all, recognized my value in the ring, in the gym, and in bringing a coterie of my doctor pals to the fights. I was an all-positive, no-negative asset, and I made a dear friend out of Angelo, the sweetest, nicest, and most beloved guy in boxing.

Angelo was a cupcake. Tough as hell in the corner, hellfire when the bout got hot, he cooled down and was easy to get along with as the fight finished

Angelo was the baby of a rough, tough Italian family of firemen, laborers, and hard brothers. He was babied. He didn't have to fight. His mother babied him; his older brothers looked after him. He grew up looking at Chris as his idol. He was in a glamorous field, boxing, which took to the kid Angelo as if he were a movie star.

When World War II began, Angie went overseas, although not in a combat unit. He met up with his older brother "Handsome" Jimmy, and they had a "good war" in France. He came home and headed for Stillman's Gym to begin his education under the watchful eye of his hero, Chris, who already had managed Midget Wolghast to a world title. Trainer Chickie Ferrara took Angelo under his wing. Angelo was a sponge. Boy, he was easy to teach. He loved the gym. You had to run the guys out. If you let him, he would sleep in the gym.

Angelo followed Chris to Norfolk, where the navy gave him one sell-out fight after another. Chris developed another champ: Ken Overlin. Angelo, all eyes and ears, took it all in. He was learning from the best.

Somewhere along the way, between New York and Norfolk, Angelo met a tall, beautiful model, a Georgia peach, a southern belle. People who knew them both didn't give little Angie a chance. Helen was 5 feet 7 inches tall and thin. Angelo was much shorter. Helen was already working as a model, making money in New York in a tough market. Angelo was starting in a humble trade: boxing corner man. The money was short, the promise for the future shaky. He was an Italian and a Yankee. Helen's family, who watched her closely, were appalled. They were totally against it. What future could there possibly be in Angelo Dundee?

The more Helen's family fought against the match, the more Helen became convinced that Angelo would make a great husband. Angelo was a nice, popular, a spiffy dresser, a great dancer, and a lot of fun. She met his family. They approved of the tall beauty, with her easy grace and pleasant laughter.

Helen never thought about the future. When you are young and in love, you expect the future to take care of itself. And of course it did. Helen says there were hard times, with scant pay, but they worked through it, as Angelo and Chris always had at least one fighter to pay the bills. As Helen admits today, it was always fun.

With the arrival of the Cubans, I really got involved. All of them spoke only Spanish. Angie spoke some pidgen Spanish, though not much. I spoke Spanish; it was my first language. I went to more than

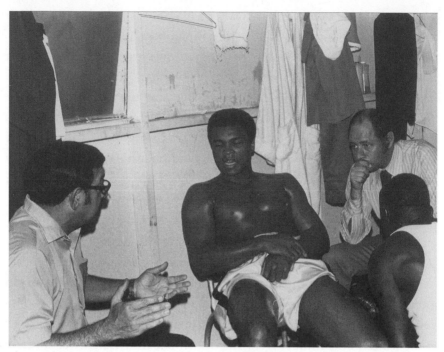

Left to right: Angelo, Ali, Ferdie, and Sarria in 5th Street Gym dressing room. Kurt Severin.

ninety fights with Luis Manuel Rodriguez and most of Florentino Fernandez' fights, and I worked with Ultiminio Ramos (the night he killed Davey Moore), Mantequilla Napoles (the night Carlos Monzon beat him half to death in Paris), and Douglas Vaillant. Boy, the Cubans were good. Angelo, who loved talent, fell in love with them. We really bonded into a team, and I finally felt like I wasn't a dopey, dilettante fan, imposing myself in the corner. I was needed and wanted. I was finally in boxing for real. It really felt good.

Then came the Ali years. Those were days of spectacular fun, days of heavy accomplishments, and days of pain and suffering.

Angelo was in a peculiar position with Ali because he was white. The Muslims said he had to go. They didn't know boxing and couldn't appreciate Angelo's value to Ali. Ali could. He was a nouveau-racist, to a point. Ali was not stupid. Ali never did anything to hurt himself as a boxer. Ali knew how much he needed Angelo, what Angelo brought to the table. Angelo, when you examine the first years, was the ring general who made Ali and matched him fight by fight until he got Liston in the ring. And then Angelo was the one who saved his ring life by not letting him quit in the fourth round of blindness. Angelo saved him. Without Angelo, there would never have been an Ali. Ali knew that, even if the others, blinded by racial hatred, didn't. Ali told them not to interfere in his ring life. Not only did he have a white manager, he also had a white doctor—me—and I would stay also. I was a different chip. The Muslims couldn't ever figure me out. First, I had a charity clinic in the black Overtown ghetto. I gave away millions in free medical care over twenty years. Ali had been my patient since he first got there at age eighteen. He was comfortable with me; I was a port in a storm. He hung out in my office.

Since I worked with all of Dundee's fighters, it was only natural to fall into the Ali entourage. I never charged a fighter—and Ali, making a million dollars a fight, wondered why I wouldn't take a dime. "So you can't tell me what to do," I answered. He understood, but most of the

Left to right: Angelo Dundee, Ferdie, and Chris Dundee. Jim Gestwicki.

Ferdie, Angelo *(center),* and Cassius Clay. Kurt Severin.

Muslims never did. All of them thought that somehow I was connected with the Mafia.

From time to time, we would come to a minicrisis that I solved all by myself. I never wanted to bring Angelo into my fight, for fear of jeopardizing his position. I was accepted as part of the treasures that Angelo brought to the table: Sarria, a valuable conditioning coach; and Pacheco, a fight doctor.

I think we helped Angelo and never hurt him. We kept quiet, did our work, and vanished when the fight was over. Ali treated me like an old friend, and we became good friends.

The sad part of the Ali story occurred at the end. After the ruthless destruction of the "Thrilla in Manila," I began to see obvious signs of deterioration in Ali's physical condition. His kidneys were beginning to fall apart. Blood and whole tubular cells passed after a fight: not a spot or two but a flood.

Then I saw a marked diminution of his reflexes in the gym. Ali no longer blocked punches easily but was getting hit by sparring partners. His jab was slowing down. No one in his camp, including Angelo, wanted to acknowledge the change.

By the time of the Earnie Shavers fight in 1977 in New York, it was remarked, "Don't worry; we'll only get him easy fights."

"Easy fight? Earnie Shavers!" The hardest puncher in the heavyweights. That was the hardest fight Ali could take!

Shavers almost knocked out Ali in the middle rounds. Ali's reputation for faking an injury saved him from a knockout but not from the king-size beating.

The New York doctor called me and told me Ali would never be approved to fight in New York again. Wearily, I agreed, but I knew that Angelo and the Muslims would not let him quit, nor did Ali want to quit.

I walked out. I was heartsick, but not because of Ali. Ali was a fighter. Fighters never want to quit, especially when they are the world champs and can make five million dollars a fight. I was heartsick because of Angelo. I didn't want to say or do anything in the press that would cast a dark shadow on Angelo. Angelo knew Ali was shot. Angelo knew Ali was taking head blows that would result in further neurological damage. He knew, because I told him so, repeatedly. But Angelo, like Chris, is part of boxing. You go on. The future doesn't matter. He can still go one more.

"Since when have you had the right to stop an Ali fight? The Muslims and Herbert have that right. You don't," I said.

Of course he couldn't. Leon Spinks, an inexperienced Marine, beat Ali on February 15, 1978, in Las Vegas over fifteen rounds. Ali took hundreds of head shots. It was a disgraceful way to blow the title.

Angelo went to the dressing room with me and Helen and said to Ali, "That's it. That's enough. You got to quit."

"You're right," said a chastised Ali, but I knew better. So did Angelo.

Brent Musberger *(right)* at Ferdie's first time as a broadcaster. Luisita Sevilla Pacheco.

Soon the trumpets were blowing for a rematch: September 15, 1978, at the Superdome in New Orleans, Louisiana. Ali beat Spinks easily. But he still took head punches by the dozen. The damage piled up, and the evidence of neurological damage was obvious to the naked eye. Ali couldn't walk straight or talk without slurring.

When I pushed Angelo to the wall, he would rationalize: "I was with him when he started, I'll be with him to the end. If I'm in the corner I can stop the fight and protect him."

You see, I had trouble with that. That was a crime. At some point, you have to jump off the boxing bandwagon and alight in the land of common sense.

That was my last hurrah with Ali. I had quit after the Shavers fight in 1977. In the first Spinks fight, I was the CBS announcer with Brent

Musberger. We earned an Emmy. By the time of the Holmes fight, I didn't even want to watch Ali at home on TV.

And that is what happened on that sad night when Larry Holmes, a former sparring partner, who did not want to beat up Ali, nonetheless did. Angelo had a chance to stop the fight in the third round but didn't, and Ali took the beating that sent him hurrying into parkinsonism.

And that was not all: later, Don King took Ali to the height of humiliation with the fight with Trevor Berbick in the Bahamas in December 1981.

Yes, Angelo was there.

No, Angelo didn't stop it.

I couldn't bring myself to talk to Angelo lest I break our happy association.

Angelo, Chris, Don King, and Bob Arum all were wrong. The money was good; the results were not.

Initially I was vilified by the Ali Circus and some of the boxing community. It had been a great twenty-five years, with lots of thrills, but

Left to right: Manny Sciacca, Bob Arum, and Chris Dundee. Jim Gestwicki.

Ferdie and Angelo *(right)* at the Olympics in Barcelona. Ferdie Pacheco Collection.

the rude awakening of the end took my heart out of being a part of the sport.

I wish I had been wrong.

I started out to make up what I thought Angelo would not say for himself. He was too modest. He won't take credit.

Now many years have passed. Angelo and I have traveled the world together in boxing. It was pure heaven.

We both continued on our respective roads: Angelo, training more world champs, and I in broadcasting, now retired from it. I considered him a close friend. He is the godfather of my daughter, Tina. More, I cannot say. In putting a worthy life in perspective, I look at it this way.

The first and most important thing in Angelo's life's list is his family: his wife and their children, son Jimmy (who inherited Helen's beauty) and daughter Terry (who has Angelo's sweet, lovable personality). Angelo and Helen raised those two jewels in a happy home. Life seemed to progress from fight to fight. They traveled the globe. They became part of the Ali Magical Traveling Circus. And all of a sudden, before we could say "Title fight!" they grew up. They got good educations and made wonderful marriages, and they gave Angelo and Helen grandchildren.

Could a life be better lived? Not many of my friends could boast such a happy life.

Next on the list came his older brother Chris. Angelo idolized Chris. He owed Chris everything.

Next in importance was unquestionably Ali. His influence and importance was gigantic. With Ali, Angelo became internationally famous.

Helen and Angelo. Angelo Dundee Collection.

After that came a mishmash of hundreds of boxers and boxing people. Angelo's boxers came to be known as "Angelo's Army." I'm a Civil War historian, so I liken them to the "Stonewall Brigade," that ferocious army that made Stonewall Jackson so feared.

Now Angelo is an actor in the movies. God bless him.

Finally, in one chapter, I have disgorged all I wanted to say about Angelo, an exceptional man. He never would.

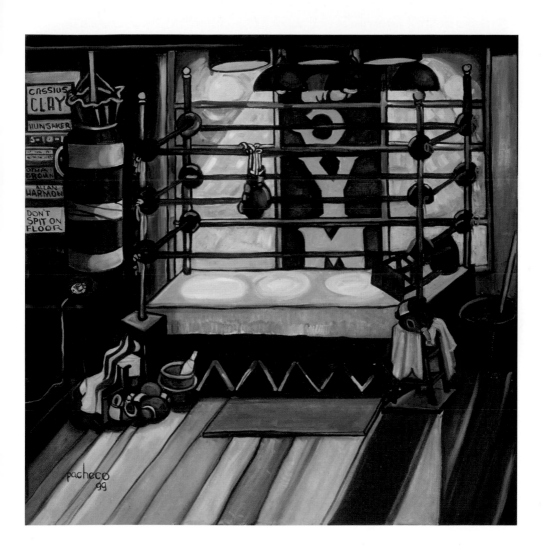

Chris Dundee

An Appreciation

Time passes, famous faces fade, important people in the community disappear from memory. One wonders why. They were such bright shining lights, the epicenter of their time. They defined their era.

At one time, boxing on Miami Beach was known worldwide. In Miami of the 1940s, 1950s, and 1960s, its epicenter was the Miami Beach Auditorium, where major league boxing took place on Tuesdays. Wrestling on Wednesdays paid the bills.

To run a successful promotion, it was necessary to have a gym to feed the need of once-a-week boxing. Here, Chris Dundee reigned as the "capo di tutti capi," the boss. His knowledge of boxing was astonishing, his connections spun all over the globe. His fingers were in every pot.

The 5th Street Gym became the University of Boxing. A trip to the gym was necessary to know boxing. On a daily basis, world-famous champions would work out next to four round pugs.

A brother, Joe, got into boxing, and Chris followed as his corner man, manager, cut man, and promoter. In no time, Chris had built a solid stable of fighters.

Chris Dundee talking to Marty Cohen at the fights. Jim Gestwicki.

Boxing in the 1950s was pretty well controlled by the Mafia, and Chris had to join the boxing union of Frankie Carbo. This enabled Chris to develop world champions and to elevate himself to promoter.

Eventually Chris moved to the navy town of Norfolk, Virginia. With Carbo's blessing, Chris built up a thriving wartime promotion.

Left to right: Tina Pacheco and Bronwyn Chovel talking with Chris Dundee at the fights. Luisita Sevilla Pacheco.

Left to right: Michael Dundee, Chris Dundee, Moe Fleischer, and trainer Billy Sullivan. Jim Gestwicki.

When World War II was over, Chris eyed the virgin territory of Miami, Florida, where small-time boxing had always done well. He saw the need for an important boxing gym and promptly opened a big gym on 5th Street and Washington Avenue. It was called the 5th Street Gym.

To help him with the gym and manage his fighters, he brought in his kid brother Angelo, who had recently been discharged from the army. It was a match made in heaven. Chris knew everything about the upside-down world of boxing: who to respect, who to fear, and who to run over. Angelo knew the rest.

Angelo was a sweet-hearted, innocent kid and genuinely loved the nuts and bolts of boxing. He also was great in the corner.

Chris went out and bought Angelo two champions: Willie Pastrano and Ralph Dupas. This acted as a magnet, and people began sending Angelo their fighters to transform into champions. Not everyone made it, but the brothers brought in hordes of fighters who thought they could be champions. The net result was that the 5th Street Gym filled up and stayed filled from the 1950s to the 1970s. In this period, Angelo

Cassius Clay and Chris Dundee. Lynn Pelham.

developed twelve world champions, including the most famous of all the 5th Street Gym alumni—Cassius Clay!

Chris and Angelo's Cuban connections to Cuco Conde and Martinez Conil, the two top Cuban promoters, paid off when Fidel Castro took over in 1960. The Cuban fighters who wound up in the 5th Street Gym included welterweight champions Luis Manuel Rodriguez and Jose "Mantequilla" Napoles, featherweight champion Ultiminio Ramos, and middleweight contender Florentino Fernandez, along with Baby Luis, Robinson Garcia, and a covey of lesser Cuban fighters. In Miami's growing Cuban community, they helped Chris sell out whenever they fought.

Chris Dundee was the unheralded brain behind all the champions of the 5th Street Gym. He made the moves and made sure that the opposition did not make any "moves" against his fighters. It was a perfect combination: Chris, the hard guy; and Angelo, the angel.

The character of Chris Dundee was delicious to observe. He was pure Damon Runyon and would fit into the cast of *Guys and Dolls.*

He had a passing resemblance to Groucho Marx, with the same kinky hairline, thick black horn-rimmed glasses, and the distinct impression that he was smoking a big black Havana cigar, although Chris did not smoke!

Chris developed a deafness, which seemed to increase when money was being negotiated. Funny stories of Chris, his deafness, and a Yogi Berra type of inverted thinking abound:

We sat in the corner sandwich shop.

Waitress: "What will you have?"

Chris: "Corned beef on rye."

Waitress: "White bread or black?"

Chris: "Yes."

Waitress: "I said, do you want white bread or black bread?"

Chris: "I said yes."

Waitress: "Mr. Dundee, I'm talking about which bread you want, bread, bread, Mr. Dundee?"

Chris: "Of course bread, how can you make a sandwich without bread?"

Chris was famous for his tightness of purse in the gym. One day he gets a long-distance call from Cleveland. His red phone in the gym had a lock on the dial. He had the only key. This is one typical exchange:

Operator: "Mr. Dundee, I have a collect call from . . ."

Dundee: "Sorry, I can't hear you."

Operator: "I'll try a different line . . . can you hear me now?"

Chris: "Sorry, the line is bad, can't hear you."

After a four-minute delay:

Operator: "Now, is it better?"

Chris: "No, I can't hear."

Exasperated operator: "Tell him it's me, Luigi Farinello, in Cleveland. I'm in a jam and I need five hundred dollars quick."

Operator: "Did you hear that, Mr. Dundee?"

With his eye on a prominent heavyweight skipping rope, Chris doesn't miss a beat.

Chris: "No, I didn't, operator."

Operator: "It's Mr. Luigi Farinello from Cleveland. He says to send him five hundred dollars now."

Chris: "I didn't hear him."

Operator: "I heard him clearly."

Chris: "Listen, lady, if you can hear him *you* loan him the money."

And he hung up, locked the phone, and ignored its insistent ringing.

Chris Dundee: The Boss

Chris had a scruffy fifty-five-year-old lady who cleaned the gym for years. Today she would be called a "bag lady." One day Willie Pastrano was the last to leave the gym, and one thing led to another, and Willie succumbed to temptation.

Chris was outraged. He yelled at Willie and reminded him that he had a beautiful wife and five children. Willie just smiled his sweet smile until Chris finally exploded. "How can thirty minutes of sin equal a lifetime of guilt?" bellowed Chris.

Willie put his head down and thought about it.

"How do you make it last thirty minutes?" he asked, and Chris gave up.

Chris had a hot black Dominican fighter, Juan Hidalgo, who was undefeated in twenty-five fights. His brother, Dario Hidalgo, had been a champion, and the kid was headed the same way. But in his way stood Termite Watkins, a tough white kid who had a lot of television exposure.

At Christmas, Chris sent Juan home to break his yearlong training. "Eat, dance, and do those other things," Chris said vaguely.

The kid returned happy, peaceful, and ten pounds overweight.

"Get in shape, kid, you're going on TV in February with Termite," Chris said casually to the kid as he came into the gym.

The kid was shocked. A maniac for conditioning, he knew that six weeks was not enough time to lose ten pounds and get in strong fighting shape. He refused. Chris insisted. The kid stood his ground. Now, Chris was tough to say no to when he got mad, and he had graduated from the same school as Blinky Palermo and Frankie Carbo, Mr. Grey, in Philly. The kid said no. Chris gets Angelo over and yells at him as if Angelo is still in short pants.

"Get in there and tell your kid he's fighting in six weeks. You're the manager, fer chrissakes, act like one."

Angie goes in. His demands do no good—strikeout. Chris is livid. "Get Sarria; tell him to train Juan like he does Ali."

Sarria goes in. The kid holds firm.

I've come to the gym and am watching in detached amusement. Chris eyes me. He knows I work the kid's corner.

"Doc, go in there and tell this kid you're going to give him the same buildup shots you give Ali before a big fight."

"What shots?" I ask, trying to get out of this.

"Make up 'what shots.' What do I know? Am I a doctor? Who are you, George Washington?"

Obediently I troop in and give it a half-hearted try. The kid is a rock and still says no.

Finally Chris's Italian temper boils over. He pushes us aside, berating us, and goes in to see the teenage boxer.

"Kid, everything being equal, there has never been in the history of boxing a white boxer who can beat an equal black boxer." Chris hit the training table so hard that the cubic zirconium on his pinkie ring fell to the floor. Raising his voice so the entire gym could hear him, Chris yelled, "Never been a white fighter that can beat a black equal fighter!"

The gym has fallen silent now. Not even a dangling participle is heard to fall. Then, the kid speaks:

"But I'm not black, Mister Dundee. I'm Dominican."

The fight did not take place. When it did, things being equal, the white fighter beat the equal Dominican fighter.

"Wouldn't have happened, if the kid only knew he was black," Chris said, shrugging his shoulders and putting the phones in the safe.

Chris loved to give old-timers from the North work. He had a small gnome of a man at the door who called himself Emmett Sully because he hung out in Sullivan Square and he liked Emmett Kelly, the clown. Emmett Sully's square moniker was Italian, but he had disclaimed being Italian since he claimed the Italians had embarrassed him by giving up all the time in World War II.

Sully charged twenty-five cents to come into the gym, fifty cents if Ali was working out, and a buck during the big Ali pre-fight workouts. He was ruthless collecting the coin. Press guys would walk in and flash their press credentials, and Sully would say, "Fifty cents, Bub."

"But I'm the press."

"Yeah! Yeah! Press my pants, you mud toitle. Come up with the coin."

Chris had him work the corner of one of our great journeymen boxers, Jerry Powers, a lightweight. Powers always saw the funny side of any eventuality.

Once the cops caught Jerry running down Miami Avenue at dawn carrying a brand new color TV set he had just taken from Sears. Now, every policeman in Miami knew Jerry Powers.

"What are you doing, Jerry?" the policeman asked.

"Road work," said Jerry, flashing his best no-front-teeth smile.

"Carrying a color TV set?"

"Yeah," said Jerry, shrugging. "I got tired of the black and white TV."

When Jerry got out of jail, they put Sully to work in his corner. Jerry was not too friendly with soap and water, and neither was Sully, so the corner was funky. But Sully liked to keep a stub of a nasty cigar in his mouth, and this one was lit.

Jerry was an experienced pro: he liked to box, and he liked to take his time. If a fight went the distance, which it often did, he was happy. This night he knocked his guy out in two rounds. Flat. Jerry didn't stop to have his hand raised by the referee. He flew out of the ring, heading for the dressing room as though his parole officer was after him.

"What happened, Jer?"

"Aw, man, I ain't going back in that corner no mo'. That Sully got some evil funk on him, and on top o' that, he be burning me with his cigar when he talks to me."

All smiles, Jerry was dressed and gone by the time Sully returned.

"I coulda made that mud toitle a champeen if they'd give him to me ten years ago," Sully announced to the press, giving them his best toothless smile.

Announcer

My favorite ring announcer was a slick-talking, one-word man, a super salesman named Frank Freeman. He had a silver tongue and a wonderful mesmerizing voice.

Twenty-five years after the first Ali-Liston fight in 1989, I was asked to do a two-hour special on the event. We took our NBC cameras to the 5th Street Gym, and I sent for Frank Freeman.

We had a top NBC crew with a talented producer named David Neal who was young and eating up all the grungy atmosphere of the gym.

Frank Freeman at the microphone, honoring Chris Dundee with a plaque. Jim Gestwicki.

Jim Bishop *(left)* and Chris Dundee. Jim Gestwicki.

He was delighted to see the spiffy Frank Freeman, then a seventy-five-year-old man, come into the gym. Freeman was still smiling, still conning with the velvet voice. After a few hugs, we got down to business.

"Frank, was the Ali-Liston—" I started to say.

"Clay-Liston," he corrected me. He was sharp; he was all there.

"Yeah. Was that the biggest fight you ever worked in your life?"

"Biggest event, never mind fight," he said, his eyes lighting up. "It was big: Jackie Gleason, Frank Sinatra, and Jim Bishop."

"Well, I'm going to ask you what the biggest event you ever worked was. Then you tell me—don't look at the camera—just tell me. And don't worry, we're on tape. So if we don't get it, we'll reshoot it."

The technicians lit him properly and fussed with his tie, and I could see a strange look coming over Frank. He looked a little trapped, a little uneasy.

Young David, stopwatch in hand, yelled, "Speed, up to speed and go."

I asked my questions and Frank froze. His eyes bulged. He said nothing.

We acted as if it was a rehearsal. We repeated it again. Same reaction. I called for water, which Frank gulped, happy to be furnished with an excuse for choking. "Throat's dry."

"Look, Frank, I am going to ask you this: Was the Liston-Clay fight the biggest event in your life? And then you say yes and if you want to add something, do so." I began on cue:

"Frank Freeman, the veteran ring announcer for twenty-five years. Frank, was the first Clay-Liston fight the greatest event of your life?"

Silence . . . a flicker of light in his eyes.

"No—World War II was bigger."

"Cut. Print. That's a wrap," said our young producer, mentally consigning that segment to the garbage can.

5

Chris Dundee's Laws of Boxing and Promotions

Enrique Encinosa

Enrique Encinosa is the acknowledged expert on the Hispanic boxing scene. A columnist, a novelist, and an author specializing in the Cuban boxers who fled from Castro, he also managed fighters and promoted fights.

When I met him he was already a legend. Chris Dundee was then in his late sixties but still promoting a dozen fight shows a year, booking fighters to Europe and Las Vegas, and running his beloved termite-infested 5th Street Gym, the house where legends trained.

Chris Dundee's boxing career stretched for seven decades, from the age of speakeasies to the age of computers. In his lifetime, Chris promoted over a thousand professional boxing shows and handled the careers of several world champions, dozens of contenders, and a small army of preliminary pugs.

When Chris Dundee became involved in boxing, people listened to a new sound called jazz, played by young gods of the horn named Armstrong and Beiderbecke. Liquor was outlawed, but all drank bathtub gin and admired the daring of Lindbergh. It was the time when Dempsey was champ, the Babe was the King of Swat, and John Barrymore had a dashing profile. Hitler was a little-known local political figure in Ger-

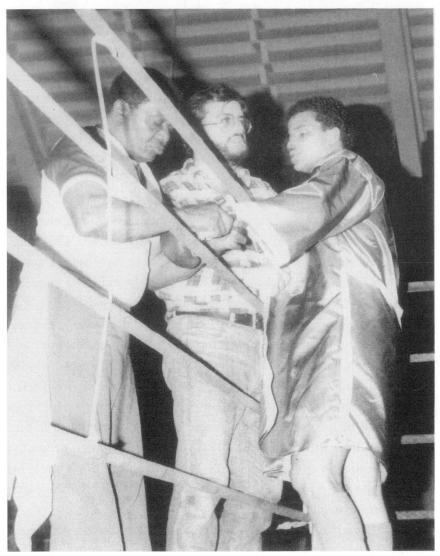

Left to right: Caron Gonzalez, Enrique Encinosa, and boxer Jose Dinamita Perez. Jim Gestwicki.

many, and the stock market crash that brought the age of economic depression had not yet cast its dark shadow over Wall Street.

By the time Dundee called it a day, the depression, a world war, and conflicts in Korea and Vietnam had concluded. Juice bars with avocado protein drinks had replaced the speakeasies, techno-rock was the new vogue sound, fax machines and the Internet were changing world communications, and Dan Marino was a seasoned football star.

In between the beginning and the end, Chris Dundee promoted fights that included the birth of the Ali legend, managed numerous world champions, and was a top booking agent.

In his lifetime, Chris Dundee knew such literati as Ernest Hemingway and Norman Mailer, smoked Cuban cigars with Errol Flynn, attended parties with George Raft and Ed Sullivan, and played cards with Rocky Marciano. At his place of business, a termite-eaten gym, the Beatles met Muhammad Ali in a "gathering of icons" moment of the 1960s.

The seven decades of boxing began when a young Chris Mirena became the boxing manager for one of his brothers, a club fighter who battled under the name of Joe Dundee. When Joe retired, Chris kept the Dundee name. Although most of his fighters were older than he was, Chris learned the tricks of the trade with the skill of a virtuoso. At the age of twenty-three, the young manager guided Midget Wolghast to a world flyweight title. Chris sailed through the Great Depression promoting club fights, managing and booking prelim boys and top-notch fighters. Crowded by New York competition, which included some totally unscrupulous characters, Chris looked for a virgin territory in which to establish his kingdom.

Chris fell in love with Miami Beach, the land of art-deco hotels, golden beaches, and exotic rum drinks. Boxing had been promoted with some success in the Magic City, but at the time Chris made his move, in the early 1950s, Miami Beach was ready for a hardworking fight impresario.

So was born the 5th Street Gym, the revered temple of sweat where the Ali legend was to be sparked, where Luis Manuel Rodriguez, Willie Pastrano, and other Hall-of-Famers plied their trade. From the mid-1940s to the early 1990s, Dundee promoted boxing, often at a loss, making up income on wrestling shows and an occasional circus troupe.

He was a real promoter. In this modern age of pay-per-view and television contracts, promotions feed on media advertising to make deals. Chris did all of that, with the title fights, the television shows, and closed-circuit theater fights plus hundreds of cheap cards to keep the fighters busy.

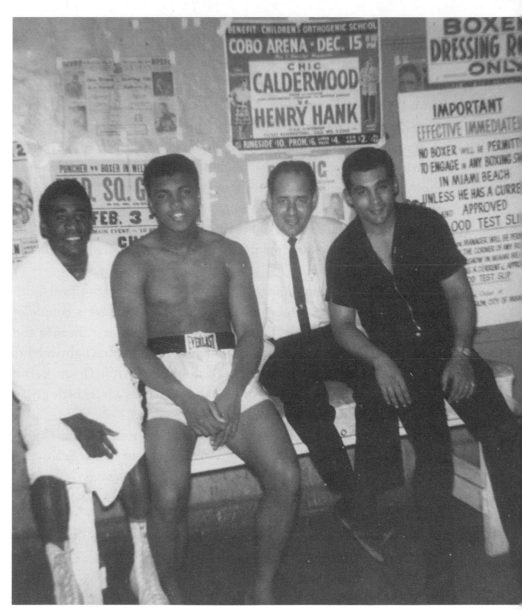

Left to right: Luis Manuel Rodriguez, Cassius Clay, Ferdie, and Willie Pastrano.
Ferdie Pacheco Collection.

"He was a hustler when it came to promoting ticket sales," the great historian Hank Kaplan remarked. "Chris would visit the track, local hotels, and all sorts of public events. Since he was so well known, many strangers would come say hello, and Chris would pitch his upcoming card. He always had a book of tickets with him and would sell them ringside or general admissions on the spot."

Dundee guided the careers of champions Ken Overlin, Ezzard Charles, "The Cincinnati Cobra," and the first Bahamian to win a world crown, Elijah Obed. Dundee promoted the first Clay-Liston bout, when the Greatest still used his slave name of Cassius Clay.

"The title fights and TV fights are easy," Chris once said. "It's the club fights with five hundred paying customers that are hard. There's no budget."

Since the budget was limited, Chris was often unable to afford fighters from other cities. The Dundee solution was to have a couple of dozen local prelim fighters fight each other over and over. In 1963 and 1964, peak years for Chris, his crew of featherweights and lightweights was made up of Jerry Powers, Sandy Seabrooke, Winston Green, Berlin Roberts, Santos Flores, and George Sawyer. This was a busy little group that fought each other over and over, for years.

Jerry Powers fought 158 fights in his all-prelim career, but almost 70 of those bouts took place in 1963–64. He fought Sandy Seabrooke twelve times, Berlin Roberts eight, Winston Green on seven occasions, George Sawyer six, and Santos Flores only five. Of Powers's 158 fights, almost 40 fights were against three opponents.

In the same two-year span, Winston Green, who faced Powers on seven prelim fights, also traded leather twice each with Seabrooke and Flores and once with Roberts.

"If two guys put up a good scrap," former lightweight contender Frankie Otero remarked, "Chris would book a rematch. If you were a prelim fighter who wanted to fight and were not too picky about your opponent, Dundee would give you work."

"Mostly he had fights," Ferdie Pacheco once told me. "Shoestring budget for some shows, but he kept it going. Even when he wasn't scheduled to fight, Jerry Powers would show up with his gym bag, and if Chris was one bout short, it would be a four-rounder with Jerry and

Left to right: Elijah Obed, Hank Kaplan, and Ferdie. Hank Kaplan Archive.

any of the other seven or eight guys like him who fought each other all the time."

I learned much about the fight game from Chris Dundee. In the early 1980s, when I was part of the promotional team of Hank Kaplan–Ramiro Ortiz in Fort Lauderdale, Chris was our consultant guru. His short statements defined situations so well that among his friends, the statements were jokingly called "Chris Dundee's Laws."

"Chris Dundee's Law on Betting," Frankie Otero remarked, "was 'Never bet against an unbeaten fighter.'"

His laws on promotion were similar pearls of wisdom gathered since the days of Dempsey and Tunney. "When you put on a card," Chris told me, "always put on your worst bout first and your best fight at the end. This way, you get the worst match out of the way while the people are sitting down or buying hot dogs and then they go home remembering the last bouts, which were the best fights."

Dundee's Law of Prelim Fights: "The perfect undercard fight is when you have two guys who like to throw a lot of punches and neither one of them can crack an egg. Then the fight goes the distance, no one gets hurt, and the fans are happy."

Dundee's Law on Heavyweights: "Anything can happen when big guys clash."

Dundee's Law on Complimentary Tickets: "Once you give a complimentary ticket to a paying customer, you will lose a paying customer forever."

Dundee's Law on Cutting Purses: "Always cut a purse. If you don't, because the kid is just making small change on a prelim fight, then six or seven fights later when you cut the purse for the first time the fighter will look at you like you are raping him. Always cut the purse. It's important the fighter understands the business relationship."

Dundee's Law on House Fighters: "Protect a house fighter but never to the point where it hurts the reputation of the promotion. Give the local fighter an edge but the house pays to see a fight. The first priority of a promoter is to put on good fights."

"Chris was really good at match making," Frankie Otero remarked. "I had a great corner with Richie Riesgo, Luis Sarria, and Ferdie Pacheco, but I owe my career to Chris. He knew how to match me. 'This guy is going to make you work hard, Frankie,' he would say, 'but if you are in shape and box him you will beat him.' Chris knew something about every fighter . . . if the guy was in shape, if he took a shot, if his reflexes were fading. Chris was very sharp. When he made matches for me with Kenny Weldon and Jimmy Trosclair, he knew they would be competitive fights, but I won them because Chris understood both my talents and my limitations as a fighter and the same for my opponents. He made me a local hero and a contender."

Dundee made significant income over the decades by booking Florida-based fighters in Europe. Local prelim boys with so-so records would fly across the Atlantic, lose to a European or British champion, and pick up a payday five times the size of a hometown stake. Chris would book fights for a ten to fifteen percent fee.

During the years when I was also match making and booking fighters, my sleep was often interrupted by a Chris Dundee call.

"Wake up," he would say. "I need a welterweight for London. Ten rounds against the British and Commonwealth champion. It pays three thousand. Can you get someone?"

"Chris," I would answer, looking at the digital numbers on the night-stand clock, "it's three o'clock in the morning."

"Not in London," Chris would answer from his Miami Beach home. "They just called me, and they need a welterweight now. See if you can get someone. I'll call you back in half an hour."

Chris was a persistent salesman who could drive a hard deal. When a hotel in the Cayman Islands staged a pro card, Dundee called to offer a fight. I had a welterweight prelim fighter with a nine-and-three re-cord that Chris, in his match-making wisdom, had figured as a pleasing opponent for a good prospect on the edge of contender status. Chris offered $800 for an eight rounder, plus expenses. I turned it down.

"Why?" Chris looked at me with a convincing countenance of stunned disbelief.

"Ralph Twinning is undefeated in seventeen fights and is a south-paw. It's a very tough fight for very short money, Chris."

"Think about it."

"The answer is no, Chris."

A month later, I was match making a card in Hialeah. Needing to complete an eight-rounder, I dropped by Dundee's small office at the Miami Beach Convention Center.

"I need a cruiser to fight Dynamite Perez," I said. "It's an eight rounder."

"The Bahamian fighters are training here now," Chris said, "and Gary Clark is experienced. We can do it for fifteen hundred."

Chris nodded his head vigorously, hoping I would nod back in agreement.

"Same deal as with Ralph Twinning," I said. "Eight hundred for eight rounds and he doesn't have to travel far to fight."

"No!" Chris answered. "This is a good fight."

"Sure it is," I answered, "an even fight that could go either way. It's good."

"A thousand," Chris said. "It's a main event."

"It's a small promotion and the money is tight."

Left to right: Chris Dunee, Dwaine Simpson, and Angelo Dundee at Thanksgiving dinner. Dwaine Simpson Collection, Brooklyn College Library.

"A thousand," Chris repeated like a mantra.

"Thanks, but I have to go make some calls," I said. "If you won't take it for eight hundred, I'll get some farm boy from Homestead to go against Perez for five hundred in a six. It won't be much of a fight, but the rest of the card is solid."

"A thousand."

"Bye, Chris."

He followed me to the parking lot.

"Nine hundred."

"Okay."

"Young man," he said, shaking my hand as he smiled, "you have learned the business."

Although he drove hard bargains and could argue with a booking agent for an hour over a fifty-dollar expense, Chris Dundee also had a warm heart. He donated money to charities, and once a year, every Thanksgiving, he would host a huge dinner for his boxing people at a local restaurant.

Sportswriter Tom Archdeacon called it a "Pug's Thanksgiving Feast," and it was a moving moment of camaraderie among men whose bond is the communion of pain in a squared ring.

Chris Dundee's Thanksgiving Dinner was attended by the successful and the destitute, by upcoming prospects and old prelim fighters with scarred eyebrows, by paunchy old men who once strutted their stuff under bright lights, when their muscles were young and supple.

It was a spectacular group. There was ancient "Sell-Out" Moe Fleischer, who had known Bat Masterson, had managed Kid Chocolate, and had trained Tom Heaney. Across from Moe sat Emmett Sully, a little man with an incomprehensible chatter and an eternal, well-chewed cigar stub at the corner of his mouth. There were also several generations of prelim fighters represented, men who talked among themselves of six hard rounds fought for meager paydays yet rejoiced in the retelling of the hard fights, wishing they could turn back the clock, to do it all over again. As many as thirty people attended the once-a-year dinner, and Chris paid the full bill.

Chris Dundee died at a nursing home in Florida in November 1998. The funeral home was packed with familiar faces: Angelo, Ferdie, Robert Daniels, Uriah Grant, Frankie Otero, Chuck Talhami, faces from the 5th Street Gym.

Tommy Torino was once a competent welterweight, a veteran of dozens of pro fights while in his teen years, a boy who grew to manhood in the gym. By 1998, Tommy had become a full-time promoter and manager, a disciple of the Chris Dundee constant hustle promotional system. Standing in front of the funeral home, looking at the crowd, Tommy looked glum. Chris had been his guru in the fight game.

"Hey, Tommy," I said. "Look at this crowd. This is Chris's last public appearance. We should have put on a couple of sixes and charged admission."

Tommy's glumness seemed to vanish. A slight smile appeared on his face.

"You know what?" he responded. "Chris would have loved it. Just loved it."

The Spring That Flows Eternal

Ali

How can I write about the joys of the 5th Street Gym without touching upon Muhammad Ali? How can I forget Ali? The press won't let you. Every month someone, somewhere in the world, wants an interview about Ali. Burdened with camera equipment, they come to my house. They lay cables all over my wooden floors, and then some bubblegum prom queen goes to her A-list question.

"How did you first meet Ali?"

Then I promptly throw them all out of the house. Once, in the middle of an excellent answer to a hard question, the interviewer's cell phone rang. "Out!" I said. "You don't belong in the profession."

So now, here I am, twenty-seven years after I walked out of Ali's life, writing something fresh and new about my many years by his side. I am forced to ask myself to remember back to Ali when he first stepped into the 5th Street Gym.

It's easier to start at the end, not the beginning.

Why is Ali so famous, so unforgettable, so darned engaging? You would think that the public would be repelled by the sight of this giant, stumbling, being led by photographer and best friend Howard Bingham to a table where he sits, dozing off, his hands shaking, as he waits for his moment to speak. Yet when he gets up, he receives a standing ovation. Pure undistilled waves of love swept over him. His flat face—once so animated—reflects nothing. But in his eyes, deep in his eyes, you see that Ali is thinking, thinking of something funny to say. He is enjoying himself. His beautiful wife, Lonnie, gets up to speak for him. What a shock: a woman speaking for Ali! It would seem unimaginable. But she speaks because he can no longer make words. Ali, the master of talk, is silent. And then it all falls into place. This is still Ali the hero, Ali the most admirable man. He has Parkinson's disease. It is ravaging his body, but as always, Ali won't quit. Won't quit! He seems to be saying, "Yes, I have Parkinson's, but it ain't gonna stop me. I'm still Ali. I'm still here. Take this Ali and accept him. I accept my penalty. Join me and we'll see it through."

And then he gets another standing ovation that lasts for ten minutes, and he sits patiently and signs every boxing glove, menu, and piece of paper. He stays. Stays until everyone is satisfied and they go home with the message he is sending:

"Yes, I saw Ali. He is funny as ever. He's Ali, champion of the whole wide world! Don't feel sorry for him, he's OK."

What is happening to Ali is the continuation of what I call Ali's luck. No matter how hard the problem, no matter how bleek the outlook, Ali seems to muddle through.

Sonny Liston. Twice. Oy. Problems? He won twice.

The Black Muslims. The death of Malcolm X. Ali's dangerous involvement. Malcolm died, Ali survived. Eventually he was thrown out of the Black Muslim movement, forbidden to use his name, and in spite of everything he survived. Still calls himself "Ali."

The "Thrilla in Manila." Joe Frazier, life-and-death in the final rounds. Frazier quits and goes to the hospital for four weeks. Ali wins and goes on an exhibition tour.

The Rumble in the Jungle. George Foreman and a nine-to-one underdog. Huge rain clouds threaten to stop the fight. Ali knocks Foreman out! Ali wins again.

Ali refuses to go to Vietnam. Thrown out of boxing. Cast out from the Muslim religion and forbidden to use his Muslim name. No employment in sight for three years. Summoning Ali's luck, he bends his head and invades the white college talk circuit, and in the end, he be-

Ali being helped to walk. Luisita Sevilla Pacheco.

comes the hero of the white yuppie generation. From traitor to patriot in three years! Ali's luck!

Even with the crushing effects of Parkinson's, he accepts a huge challenge. If he fails, it would be his worst defeat. Ali is asked to run up a long flight of stairs, carrying a huge Olympic torch to light the fire for the Atlanta Olympics. How he did that I'll never know. I cried for fifteen minutes after Ali did that. "Why am I surprised?" I asked after I composed myself. "It's Ali's luck."

And through it all he has maintained his sparkling, devilish sense of humor.

At a Mike Tyson fight, he came by to hug me. He held me tight and whispered in my ear, "You're still my ghetto nigger." I laughed. God, he was referring to something that had happened twenty-five years ago.

Ferdie talking to Ali in the makeup trailer of the movie *Ali* with Ferdie's granddaughter Alexis Baram *(far right)* and daughter Tina Pacheco listening. Luisita Sevilla Pacheco.

Ali was ensconced in a luxury Fontainebleau Hotel suite with eight hangers-on lying around calling room service, placing long-distance telephone calls, and in general abusing Ali's hospitality. Seeing me come in, Ali got an idea.

"Hey, Doc, you still got that little ghetto clinic? Is Ms. Mabel still with you?"

I nodded.

"I'd like to come visit the clinic."

"Yeah, let's us go to the ghetto," said one of the vultures, amused by the idea.

"No. Just Ali. No entourage, no limo. No press. Just Ali alone," I said gruffly.

"Huh? We come from the ghetto," one of the entourage said.

"There ain't one ghetto nigger in here except me. I'm down there giving away medicine from eight in the morning till eight at night. Free. You guys haven't ridden through the ghetto in a limo since you crawled on the Ali Circus Train."

Of course Ali whooped and hollered and clapped his hands in glee.

"That's right! Doc's right. He's the ghetto nigger here. He's the oliest one that has the right to call himself a ghetto nigger. I'll go tomorrow morning. Is nine OK?"

"OK, but no entourage. No TV or press. Just you. And don't bring a bag of cash and pass out hundred-dollar bills. Just sit by my desk and chat and hug them. That's all."

The next day I left my hospital rounds early to be there at 9 a.m., when Ali was to show up. I was sure he was coming but not sure how it would turn out.

Sure enough, there was a mob on the streets, blocking all of 10th Street. Parked by my office was a gigantic ABC television truck, a large cable going through the front door. And there was Ali, microphone in hand, in front of a handheld camera filming away.

"See this here clinic. It's too small. It's dirty. It smells bad. It's not good enough for my people. We need better clinics. We can't stand for this."

I grabbed him and took him into my office and proceeded to chew him out: "This office was good enough for you when you came here as a kid, when all of us pitched in to help you win the title.

"This is the ghetto clinic. You know why it smells bad? Because people come straight from work, after eight hours in the hot sun, to be treated. They don't have time to take a shower. And guess what? They smell bad. It ain't fancy, because they don't want 'fancy'—they want familiar. They want a 'ghetto office' where they feel at home."

Properly chastised, he sat down, and we began to see patients.

It was many years after, yet in Las Vegas he still saw me as a ghetto nigger!

To return to those golden early years in the 1960s, I'll start at the beginning.

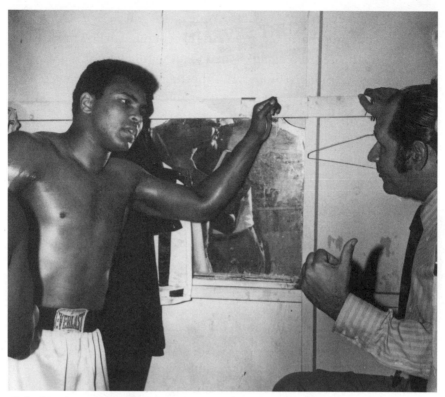

Ali and Ferdie in the dressing room. Kurt Severin.

Chris Dundee called to say he was sending Ali over for a cold shot. The kid had been placed at the Mary Elizabeth Hotel—a den of iniquity, filled with pimps, whores, drug dealers, and thieves.

Angelo knows all there is to know about how to handle a corner in a title fight, but the rest of the world floats by him as if it were all unimportant and irrelevant. Angelo had no idea where he had put the innocent kid.

Of course, Ali at nineteen years old was a sprightly bouncing ball of good humor and braggadocio. All that he knew was that he was going to win the world title. Considering that the world champion of the time was an unbeatable, gigantic assassin named Sonny Liston, people in the sports world found this talky, brash, loud-mouthed kid a joke: "Boy, wait till Sonny gets this kid in the ring!" Ali just stepped up, with his noise and the jive. Boy, was he fun to be around.

Ms. Mabel, my faithful nurse, all business, came in with a solemn look on her face.

"I don't know what it is, but Mr. Dundee said he's one of his fighters." She shook her head. "My, he sure is loud!"

I laughed at her reaction. She was probably the only one in the ghetto to not know who Cassius Clay was.

"Is he tall and good-looking?" I asked.

"Sho' is tall, good-looking, and crazy. That chile either gonna be locked up in the crazy house, or he gonna be the heavyweight champion of the world."

To see this jewel of a boxer for the first time was really a shock. He was six feet three inches tall, sleek and smooth, perfectly proportioned, with beautiful tone of skin. Although he was truly blessed with facial beauty, he didn't seem to notice it but used his beauty as a joke. "Ain't I pretty?" he would say, mincing his words, sort of making fun of himself. He was charming and adorable, and in a minute he had conquered the whole office, including Ms. Mabel and me.

Getting him to sit still was another matter. He ran around in a circle, his pants down around his knees as Mabel, syringe poised, chased him, talking to him as she would to a naughty child.

"Sit still, boy! You too big to be running around."

Finally, when the shot was given, she broke out into a relieved grin.

"You good. You the champion of shots." He hugged a flustered Ms. Mabel.

It was time for me to go to the 5th Street Gym, and I offered him a ride in my Cadillac Eldorado with the top down.

"No, thanks. I'm running to the gym."

"That's about four miles," I said.

"And then, I run from the gym back to the ghetto. Only I run it backward."

"Why? That's a long way, especially after a full gym workout."

"It's the way I fight. Going backward. My legs got to be tough to take it."

"Hmm. You know, that boy just might be the next heavyweight champion of the world," I thought to myself.

THE EXPERTS

The gray men of the 5th Street Gym shook their heads in disapproval.

"The kid drops his left hand when he jabs. Gonna get killed."

"The kid pulls back from a punch. Gonna get killed."

"The kid keeps his left down low, by his legs. Gonna get killed."

"The kid closes his eyes when he sees a big punch coming. Gonna get killed."

"The kid dances all the time. Nobody can keep that up. Gonna get killed."

All that was true, but none of it bothered Ali. Many years later, at the end of his career (after he had fought Frazier three times and Norton three times), Eddie Futch (the trainer who had worked their corner) put it succinctly into perspective: "Ali wins because he shows you all his errors and defects and then when you come in, taking advantage of those defects, he kills you with his counterpunching and his size."

It was a bitter pill for them to swallow, but Ali was truly a sensational fighter. Big, tough, fast, and superintelligent—and he wouldn't quit! Angelo was the first and I think the only one to understand Ali inside the ropes. Outside the ropes was none of Angelo's business. Ali turned Muslim; it was a surprise to Angelo. Ali married Sonji; it was a surprise to Angelo. Ali's personal life wasn't Angelo's business.

But inside the ring, Angelo had a straight pipeline to Ali's brain. Knowing that Ali didn't like to be told boxing advice, Angelo would tell him the opposite of what he wanted done, and Ali would respond exactly with what Angelo really wanted. They were a great team. Ali is so overwhelmingly his own man that you can't see where Angelo fits in. But he does.

At the beginning, the Louisville group of millionaires who financed Clay's early career wanted to hire Angelo. The deal was $150 a week, or 50 percent of the fee. Of course, Angelo relied on his older brother Chris for business advice. Chris, remember, was a son of the Great Depression. His philosophy was always to take the money up front rather than later on down the line. So Chris cut the worst deal since the Indians sold Manhattan for a dollar. Chris took $150 a week, which figured to $75 a week for each brother and no back money.

After Ali won the title, the Muslims muscled in. Out went the Louisville group and in came the gangsters from Chicago. Luckily, they did not know a thing about boxing. Ali, despite having his head filled with racist claptrap, was shrewd enough to know that he needed Angelo Dundee, Luis Sarria, and Ferdie Pacheco. Ali stood up for his boss like a rock. We lasted until he quit fighting. What the money distribution was, don't ask.

Once, in the Shavers fight, the last one I was to work, I got a message that Herbert Muhammad, Ali's manager, didn't want me to get up in the ring at the introductions. Why? Because at the previous fight in

Ferdie, Ali, and Drew Bundini Brown. Howard Bingham.

Munich, I was standing beside the Marine honor guard with the flag beside us and Ali came gliding by as the national anthem started. Ali stopped, right beside me. The TV cameras showed Ali, Dr. Pacheco, and the flag for three straight minutes. The Black Muslims reacted with an outpouring of wrath. Who was that white face next to Ali? (This was after seventeen years of the white face next to Ali.) That was almost the straw that broke the camel's back.

Then I went into the dressing room and found a Muslim man telling me that Herbert didn't want me to use the drugs I use on Ali's knuckles to deaden them—but had brought his own to use.

I had just bought fresh bottles of the drugs from an apothecary in New York. The bottle Herbert had provided had a faded label and looked murky.

"No way," I said. "It's my way or I go back to the hotel and watch the fight from there." Imagine, if I were to inject this stuff and things went bad. I'd have hell to pay.

Ali did it his way. He never wanted showdowns. He couldn't go against Herbert. So he waited until it was time, and we went into the bathroom. I took Youngblood, a Muslim of convenience, in as my witness. Ali said, "Give me the usual stuff." He threw the Muslim crap into a trash can.

As it turned out, he needed the good stuff. Shavers almost beat him. Actually, he had Ali knocked out, standing up, but Shavers had succumbed to the Ali mystique. He thought Ali was bluffing. He wasn't. The bell saved him.

This fight was also important to prove how insignificant it was for the boxers to know whether they are ahead on points. NBC had decided to announce the scores after each round. With just a tiny bit of effort, we could have had our man in the dressing room, standing by a television. A runner could get the score to Angelo. No one thought of it! Angelo was always wary of Madison Square Garden decisions, though we were about even. So he sent Ali out to do or die, a 100-percent effort, with the ever-dangerous Earnie Shavers.

Why was it such a mistake? Because the score announced on the NBC telecast had Ali ahead by four points! There was no need to fight at all. And that last round was a barn burner, which Ali, by the way, won.

Whew!

Although this is a book about the 5th Street Gym and Chris Dundee, it is hard to write about Ali without touching on his gigantic career. It is not something you can write around. He was huge.

His influence on the 5th Street Gym was as big as his career. It became the epicenter of the boxing world, the Mecca of boxing. When Ali was training, the gym filled with champions sharing the spotlight.

When Ali was a kid with no fights, Ingemar Johansson came in to train for Floyd Patterson. He asked Chris to send him a kid to spar with. He needed a speedy kid to imitate Floyd's speed.

In no time, the kid was back. Ingemar attached a note: "Take this kid and stick him up your ass. I asked for speed, not lightning."

Angelo once wanted to see if the kid was as fast as he looked, so he put him in with Willie Pastrano, the fastest guy in our gym and the light heavyweight champion of the world.

Willie lasted one round, took his gloves off, and got out of the ring. He handed the gloves to Angelo.

"Here, you go in and get slapped silly by this kid. I've had enough."

We saw the kid grow and grow every day in the 5th Street Gym. From Luis Manuel Rodriguez he learned his pinpoint left jab and the hook off the jab. He admired Luis's patented shoe-shine, which was a machine-gun, two-fisted body attack. He imitated Luis's gliding in a circle, popping stinging jabs as he went. Ali took Pastrano's beautiful footwork. Every day you could see Ali learn, absorb, sharpen his style. He was good to start with, but every day he was a little better.

Slowly the word got around. The crowds in the 5th Street Gym grew. Sully raised the price to a dollar. Pretty soon Sully could afford to go to the dog track every night to hustle old ladies.

When things went well, Chris increased the speed of his activities, and he hummed continuously. He was manic with happiness. Of all the champions he and Angelo had found, finally they had stumbled on "The One."

After Liston, when Angelo survived a coup to ax him, the Black Muslims offered the Dundee brothers a deal. Of course, it was very light, very insulting. Ali owed everything to Angelo, specifically, and to Chris and the 5th Street Gym generally. The offer was insulting enough to quit and walk away.

But here is where Chris Dundee was so important. Chris told Angelo, "Stick to him. This kid is going to be here for years. The price will come up. Where else are you going? This is the heavyweight champion and the biggest attraction in sports."

How right Chris was. In my opinion, they never paid Angelo anywhere near what he was worth. They would throw $50,000 at a comic to put Ali on a diet, another $50,000 to a Muslim doctor who almost killed him in the Holmes fight, but Angelo was always paid low. And then, when you compute Angelo's value, you have to understand that he brought with him a veteran fight doctor (me) who refused to be paid, so they got two top men for one fee. And Angelo brought the faithful Luis Sarria, master conditioner, who likewise never got what he was worth. Many of the hangers-on got more than Sarria. So Angelo's team was above and beyond what Angelo himself was worth, and still he was never paid even what he was worth.

But Angelo was a softy who fell in love with boxing excellence. Just to be part of the Ali Circus was all Angelo wanted. He didn't feel cheated or insulted; he knew it wasn't Ali's say-so. It was the way of the Black Muslims. Herbert Muhammad and his gang could steal hundreds of thousands while Angelo got bubkes. But Angelo got the pleasure and created his huge reputation because of Ali. Angelo ended up with twenty world champions. In the end, I think, in my book, Angelo won the fight.

What was an Ali 5th Street Gym workout day like? Other fighters came early so they would have space. Tourists showed up and sat in the row of theater seats. At twelve noon, a buzz outside heralded Ali's arrival. As soon as his handsome head appeared over the top step, people would start applauding. Ali went by them as if they weren't there. No one tried to touch him or talk to him. He put on his gear and went through his warm-up. Then he would glove up and get in the ring, warming up by going round and round in never-ending circles. The three-minute bell would sound. Angelo would put on his helmet, Sarria would grease his face. The sparring partner would come in, and at the bell, there would be three excellent rounds of boxing. The crowd got excited. Once the sparring partner got tagged, he dropped to one knee. The crowd went wild. Ali quietly helped the sparring partner up, said a few comforting words, and let him out of the ropes. Enough for him. Next!

The rounds over with, Ali would go to where the audience was, hang his huge arms on the top rope, and begin a monologue that was as good as that of any comedian. The audience roared, writers scribbled happily, and a good time lasted half an hour. Then Sarria got him on the table and rubbed him with his special oil.

And then, as quickly as it had started, it was over. Ali left the crowd, who were still clapping and laughing as they followed him out.

Then Angelo, Sarria, and I gathered the trainers, writers, and visitors with us and went to the Puerto Sagua Restaurant, where the Cuban cuisine was succulent, the espresso powerful. Upman cigars filled the room with their rich aroma. The conversation was wild, laughter rang out, and then we went back to work, happy to be part of Ali's world.

And another great day ended for us of the 5th Street Gym family. That went on for twenty years, though it seems like just a few minutes. As Chris Dundee often said, "What do you expect? It's boxing."

The 5th Street Gym

Howard Kleinberg

Howard Kleinberg's early life in Miami was rocky. He enlisted in the United States Marine Corps Reserve in 1951. He stayed a Marine until 1953, when a letter arrived at his house saying he was being drafted into the army! He bid farewell to the Marines and joined the army, where he stayed for two more years. It wasn't the swift start he had envisioned for himself, but he was a tough nut and he had his eye on his goal, journalism.

He started writing sports for the *Miami News* and was so good at it that in no time he was elevated to sports editor. He was a very good executive sports editor because he genuinely loved sports and had an eye for talent. He brought good writers to the *Miami News,* and its sports page was one of the best in state. Eventually this led to a promotion to managing editor, a position he held until he was forced to retire with the folding of the *Miami News.*

His zest for life, a blazing good sense of humor, and his ability to feel out a good story made him a great writer. He loved the 5th Street Gym, and his chapter shows his love for the decrepit old gym.

When first I came onto the local boxing scene, there was not yet a 5th Street Gym; Chris and Angelo Dundee had not yet put their imprint on the fight game here. Most of the fighters trained in Miami, at the Magic City Gym on Southwest Sixth Street and Second Avenue—on the river.

Left to right: Howard Kleinberg, Ferdie, and Dr. Howard Gordon. Ferdie Pacheco Collection.

Matches were being held at the now-gone Coral Gables Coliseum and at several small venues in downtown Miami with dubious headliners such as Honey Chile Whipple (who had a day job washing dishes at a Miami Beach eatery named Mammy's) and Snooks Howard, a small disaster whose principal offensive weapons were spittle and his teeth. There were headliners of greater quality as well—fighters such as Bobby Dykes and Billy Kilgore—but the most memorable were the most outrageous.

That all changed in 1950 when the brothers Dundee arrived to begin promoting boxing matches at the Miami Beach Auditorium, now known as the Jackie Gleason Theater of Performing Art. Older brother Chris was the promoter; his claim to fame was as the manager of former ranked middleweight champion Ken Overlin. Angelo, at first, stayed mainly in the background, training fighters.

For his first match at the Beach, Chris put together Dykes—a future challenger for the welterweight title—and a journeyman fighter named Aldo Minnelli. As a (very) young sportswriter for the *Miami Daily News,* I covered the fight—and wound up down at the Miami Beach police station. This came about because of two misunderstandings: one, the guard at the door of Bobby Dykes's dressing room after the fight could not believe that such a young kid was the boxing writer and denied me admission (three times); and, two, the young sports writer did not understand that the guard in civilian clothes really was a Miami Beach off-duty cop. The latter came to light when I threw a fist in his face. It was Chris Dundee himself who came down to the station to clear up matters.

Chris Dundee was a promoter's promoter. There was not a fight he booked that he did not try to convince me (and Lee Evans of the *Miami Herald*) that this was a match made in heaven. I don't recall that Chris ever had a press agent, as he always personally delivered by hand to our newsroom announcements of upcoming matches. In later years, his son Michael often would do it.

The brothers Dundee soon expanded their operations to what has become known as the 5th Street Gym, a large expanse of space sitting above a drugstore, with its entrance on 5th Street off Washington Avenue. In no time, Chris and Angelo got the place to smell just right—that sour pungency that seemed to waft off the screen at showings of *Rocky* and *The Harder They Fall.*

The fact that Chris was a consistent fight promoter (few weeks elapsed without shows) and that Angelo was gathering in a stable of brilliant young fighters (mostly from Cuba) brought the 5th Street Gym into local prominence; it even brought over Beau Jack, the old lightweight champ, who had drifted to shining shoes, first at the Fontainebleau Hotel, then at the 5th Street Gym. Despite his humble situation, Jack greeted one and all with a great smile as they reached the top of the stairway to the second floor.

Before Muhammad Ali/Cassius Clay arrived on the scene, the gym was playing host to the brilliant Angelo Dundee stable: the hard-swinging Florentino Fernandez; the waterbug-like Luis Manuel Rodriguez, who went on to the welterweight championship before falling victim

Douglas Vaillant.
Enrique Encinosa
Collection.

to alcohol; and the promising Doug Vaillant, who never fulfilled his promise and, tragically, later hanged himself. (Vaillant's manager, by the way, was none other than Bernard Barker, who later went on to fame as being one of the Watergate burglars.)

By the time the 5th Street Gym became prominent, I had moved on to other things: first, the Korean War, and then as executive sports editor of the *Miami News*. No longer did I have to climb the steps to that pungent second floor: I assigned others to do it, good sportswriters like John Crittenden, Al Levine, and Tommy Fitzgerald.

When Clay/Ali began training there, the 5th Street Gym became one of Miami Beach's favorite tourist attractions. If memory serves

Ali loosening up. Luisita Sevilla Pacheco.

World champions *(left to right)*: Abe Attel, Barney Ross, Joey Maxim, Rocky Marciano, Tom Heeney, Max Schmelling, Joe Louis, Solly Kreiger, Petey Scalzo, Beau Jack, Georgie Abrams, Petey Sarron, and Bobby Dykes. Hank Kaplan Archive, Brooklyn College Library.

me, nonaffiliated people (tourists) had to cough up fifty cents to climb the steps, be greeted by Beau Jack, and then watch some of boxing's greatest names train. The list of champions and future champions who trained there is lengthy. So popular was the gym that even the Beatles went there to have their pictures taken with Clay/Ali.

I did step down from my roost to do day-to-day coverage of Floyd Patterson's training for the Miami Beach Sonny Liston championship fight that never took place. That was because I was very fond of Patterson. We both had the pleasure of being refused service at a chili joint on Bird Road because of the color of Floyd's skin. We were somewhat linked by that civil rights experience.

Although not covering boxing anymore, I stayed close to the Dundees, principally because Chris knew that my being executive sports editor would help get him more space and prominence in our pages.

For reasons that are still unclear to me, Chris bought a bowling alley in Miami, near the entrance to the MacArthur Causeway. It was a shabby place at best, opposite the Sears Roebuck site that has since become the Adrienne Arsht Center for the Performing Arts. In his way, he lured my wife and me down there to bowl a few frames, and before we knew it, Chris had bowling balls and shoes made for us.

Personal experiences with Chris could always be exciting and were sometimes frightening. I recall ever so vividly that at times we all would go over to the Noshery in the Saxony Hotel after the fights. I was in no hurry to get back to the paper because mine was an afternoon paper and I didn't have to get my story in until around 6 a.m.

So we went to the Noshery. One night, after a fight, my wife and I were sitting having ice cream while Chris was at another table with a white-haired man who kept looking my way—probably at my wife.

When I called for the check, the waitress told me that the white-haired man had picked it up. I waved for Chris to come to my table. "Who's that man?" I naively asked.

"Why, that's Frankie Carbo," Chris responded matter-of-factly.

"Frankie Carbo?" Naïve as I may have been at the time, that name was known to me—known as that of a mob captain with, reportedly, plenty of notches on his gun. I ever so weakly waved a thank-you at Carbo, then told Chris that it was an awful thing to allow to happen to me.

For Chris, it was a shrug of the shoulders. Chris crossed many bridges in his lifetime. Some led to bad places, some went the other way. Regardless, Chris Dundee remained a lovable guy—even when he had to shut down the gym. To this day, I run into Angelo from time to time—when he isn't teaching Russell Crowe to make like Jim Braddock.

All these years later, the memory of Chris is deeply embedded—on a shelf in our garage, where my wife continues to sequester her Chris Dundee bowling ball, although she hasn't used it in thirty or so years.

8

Chris Dundee and the Ali Circus

When Chris first saw Ali (when he was still known as Cassius Clay), he was impressed by the kid's size and perfect body. He watched Clay work out, and he saw what all the gray men of the gym saw: a very fast heavyweight with welterweight speed. A boy who pulled back from a punch, closing his eyes. A boy who held his left hand very low, down around his hip. And a boy who moved so fast that he would surely not be able to keep it up for ten rounds and would never punch *hard*.

Angelo, who was the last word on evaluating a fighter, saw it differently. He saw a most unusual kid with faults that he seemed to know how to turn to his advantage. A dynamo of physical energy (seemingly inexhaustible) and a rare intelligence for the ring. In short, a miracle, a one-of-a-kind future champion. Angie fell in love.

Cassius Clay started out fast, and he accelerated. One after another, opponents fell. Clay, full of fun, started making up doggerel about his opponents. Then he began predicting the round he would knock out his opponents. Angie was perfect in picking the opponents. They got harder and harder, and Clay produced!

One fateful night in Las Vegas, Clay went to see Gorgeous George wrestle. They had a lot in common. The wrestler sat him down and gave him these solid tips:

1. Always dress in all *white;* this will drive the racists crazy. They will hate you.
2. Be brash, bold, and outrageous. Always predict your opponent's defeat.
3. Be vain: brag about your good looks.
4. Try to make the racists hate you. Remember, they will buy more tickets hoping to see you *lose.*

Cassius Clay took that and whipped it into an act. Gorgeous George was exactly correct.

That constitutes the first segment of the Ali story. The simple, uncomplicated, childlike frolic ascended the ranks of boxing. The target became Sonny Liston, who soon moved into view.

At the Doug Jones fight in New York, Clay had permitted a New York hustler named Drew Bundini Brown to join his corner. What he represented to Clay was comic relief, comradeship with a black man, and a comic, semiserious, mystical power arising from a spiritualism that was clearly phony. Bundini's one saving grace was that Sugar Ray Robinson had once taken him in and permitted him to work a fight. Bundini—a hedonist, alcoholic, drug addict, womanizer, and con man—somehow worked his way into Clay's heart and stayed throughout Ali's entire career.

Cassius Clay and Bundini then launched on a sophomoric practical-joke campaign to draw out Sonny Liston. Only one man in America believed Cassius Clay to be ready to take on Liston when Clay beat the ancient Archie Moore. The boxing writers said, "Must be that Archie needs the money"; no one could bring himself to believe in Cassius Clay. He was fun, he was flash, but he wasn't "no serious contender."

Chris, as we have noted, had a deep connection with Frankie Carbo and "the boys." He had the ability to make the Clay-Liston fight happen, because everyone knew Liston was well connected, at one time even managed by Blinky Palermo.

Eventually, Liston grew tired of being chased around the country by the bold Cassius Clay. Chris was able to put up the money through his Miami connection with Bill McDonald, a millionaire sportsman, and find an ideal location, the new Miami Beach Auditorium. The money was big for both fighters and the odds prohibitive. It opened at 8–1 for Liston, and there was a big price for it to end in a first-round knockout by Liston.

The 5th Street Gym was the focal point of attention for the entire six weeks that training went on. For us, it was a carnival. Packed crowds showed up daily. Cassius Clay, presented with a standing-room-only crowd every day, put on a sensational show. "Boy, this kid can sell!" said Chris.

Ferdie and Ali on an early morning walk in front of the Essex House in New York City. Luisita Sevilla Pacheco.

Ali jumping rope at the 5th Street Gym. Kurt Severin.

Ali would come in, loosen up, do the light bag (very fast), skip rope expertly at high speed and with a lot of grace, and seldom hit the heavy bag. Some thought that his *not* punching the heavy bag was a hint that he wasn't going to go to the body. Then he put on headgear and worked out with his sparring partners, one of whom was his brother, Rudy. Then came the star turn. He would go to the ropes, put his hands on them, hook one foot on the bottom strand, and speak, always ending up in a harangue on Liston. Clay left them laughing, and you felt he could easily do fifteen minutes more. It was fun!

A VISIT FROM
SONNY LISTON
1963—

Liston, in the City of Surfside Creation Center, worked out by the ocean and drew a thin crowd. That was because he barely worked. He started each day by saying, "I don't know why I'm training. I'm knocking the chump out in the first round."

Then he did a lumbering slap rope to a slow-tempo tenor sax solo by Erskine Hawkins called "Night Train." Then Willie Reddish, an old corner guy, would throw a medicine ball at Liston's abdomen. Considering that Clay *rarely* punched to the belly, it should have seemed unnecessary to toughen his abdomen. Then he did minor exercise on the table and he was gone. Unlike Clay, he never talked to the crowd, disdained photo opportunities, and seemed anxious to leave.

They were preparing for two different fights.

Meanwhile, down deep in the Overtown ghetto, my spies informed me that Rudy, Clay's brother, had been converted to the Black Muslim faith by Captain Sam, a good recruiter who hung out at Red's Barbershop, the hub of the ghetto.

Cassius Clay was bothered and confused by how he was greeted after he won the gold medal in the 1960 Rome Olympics. He was an innocent, charming boy who never looked for trouble and went on his way

Ali and his daughter, Laila; Ferdie and his daughter, Tina. Luisita Sevilla Pacheco.

depending on his charisma, charm, and athletic accomplishments to get along in the South.

He was shocked to find that none of his accomplishments excused him from the rigid, harsh, and unfair rules of segregation in the South and in some parts of the North as well. It annoyed him. It bothered him, but in the South of the 1960s, there was no way to beat it.

Rudy brought home the Muslim rap, with a stack of *Elijah Speaks* newspapers and literature. Clay read it and was hooked, and Captain Sam reeled him in too. It was a big catch!

The Black Muslims were born in an Atlanta penitentiary, where the Honorable Elijah Muhammad was spending a few years. He gathered about him a tough core of SS-like storm troopers called the Fruit of Islam. They set loose on Chicago to bust a few heads, run a few protection rackets, and expand into a legitimate religion of hate and violence. They did very well.

Cassius Clay bought the whole rap. This was what he had hoped to hear was possible: "Black is best." "Black is beautiful." Exactly!

I saw the transformation in Clay as he came to my office from time to time. I called Chris, who did not seem interested in Clay's religious preferences. Angelo, even more unconcerned, hid behind his mantra: "I ask him to do boxing things in the gym. What he does *outside* the ring, I don't care." Oh, brother!

This tiny grain of sand grew into a boulder as the Muslim army moved in. Clay then had a house, and the neighborhood rocked with Muslim tapes: "Kill the white devil!"

Chris was the first to start listening to me. Then Bill McDonald, a millionaire sportsman, started to react violently. He mentioned, in passing, that if this Muslim thing wasn't resolved he was pulling his money out. Chris *really* started to pay attention.

First he talked paternally to Clay. Chris knew better than to talk against the Muslims, so he took a tack called "cut your losses."

"Look, I'm not asking you to change anything regarding religion. You do what you want to do. I'm just asking you to *delay* announcing it by one week. Wait until after the fight and then announce anything you want."

The Muslims had an agenda. Clay was a huge conduit to a national spotlight. Most of America did not know what the Black Muslims were, and this would tell the *world* who they were. They knew that the word had to be passed *before* the fight. If Clay lost, who would care what he was? And, make no mistake, they all thought he was going to lose to the big, bad, ugly bear, Sonny Liston.

Ferdie *(far left)* as Drew Bundini Brown puts on Ali's glove with Youngblood looking on. Luisita Sevilla Pacheco.

Each side upped the ante, and both sides were intractable in their position. Time was running out.

Bill McDonald and Chris decided to throw down the gauntlet and call Clay's home.

"If Cassius Clay says he is a Muslim, the fight is *off,*" Dundee announced in the *Miami Herald.*

Clay, his house literally bursting with Muslims from Chicago and turning to the brilliant Malcolm X for advice, decided to get on his bus and go home. The bus loaded up. Even Bundini got on the bus. I watched and couldn't believe that a young man who had worked so hard to achieve a goal would walk away because a dangerous sect ordered him to. Sonny Liston and the quest for the heavyweight championship meant too much for Cassius Clay to walk away just like that.

"Wait till after the fight," Chris said, keeping in mind the Old English doggerel, "Winners sing and dance. Losers do whatever the fuck they want."

Once Liston had knocked out Clay, no one would care what he became.

Somehow, cooler heads prevailed. Yes, Clay would shut up and wait till after the fight. Meanwhile, the week-long battle had made every paper in the world, and there weren't many boxing fans around the globe who didn't know that Cassius Clay had now become Muhammad Ali! With everyone satisfied, the fight was on.

First there was the weigh-in. Liston, who came with Joe Louis in his corner, was almost bored by the whole thing.

We came with Sugar Ray Robinson, who, along with Angelo, tried to tell Cassius Clay how serious this all was, how the heavyweight championship was a holy rite. It was serious.

"Uh, huh," said Clay, and as soon as he hit the door he shouted, "I got you now, you big, ugly bear!"

"Rumble, young man, rumble!" Bundini joined in with Clay.

In what can best be described as a hysterical charge, Clay, Bundini, Angelo, and Robinson advanced on an amazed Sonny Liston. Ali stood nose to nose and snarled, "I gotcha now, Sonny!"

They weighed in. Sonny seemed surprised and impressed to note that Ali was *much* taller and bigger. No one thought Cassius was so big until he stood before you. Then you saw it. Cassius was BIG!

The doctor, Dr. Robbins, took Clay's blood pressure. I was standing beside him. "Here, listen to this." It was 210/180! Phenomenal. A New York writer who hated Clay asked, "Does that indicate that Clay is scared to death?" Lacking any other answer, Dr. Robbins said, "Yes, and if he is like that at fight time, the fight is off."

Immediately I was pressed into service. I was to take blood pressures every hour until fight time. Visions of lawsuits floated in the sky. We drove to the little house. In the limo, the first blood pressure fell to normal, 120/80. Dead-on normal. "Why did you do that?" I asked.

"Sonny is a jailbird. Convicts are scared of only one man: a crazy guy. And now, Sonny thinks I am crazy."

That would factor into the second fight, where Sonny went down and wouldn't get up because Ali was standing over him and "you *never know* what a crazy guy will do."

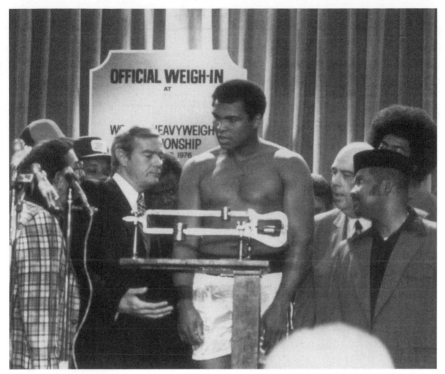

The Ali-Norton weigh-in. *Left to right*: Angelo Dundee, PR man John X. Condon, Ali, Commissioner Marvin Cohn, and Herbert Muhammad. Luisita Sevilla Pacheco.

We stayed up all afternoon. "Death to the white devils" was chanted hour after hour. Angelo and I looked at each other with a weak smile. Meanwhile I had five thousand dollars to bet on Ali, at nine to one, and I couldn't get out to bet on the fight.

We went to the auditorium, and we were locked into the bathroom locker room, Angelo, Sarria, and me. Then Bundini, Rudy, and, of course, Ali. The tension was thick. The door wasn't to be opened to anyone. Rudy was assigned the taped water bottle. He was to never take his eye off of it, so that it couldn't be drugged. By whom? Ali didn't say. Certainly not Sarria, Bundini, or me. Then perhaps Angelo? He was Mafia, was the common thought. Hardly likely, but . . .

Being locked up until fight time caused me to lose my big bet. Forty thousand dollars (or the equivalent, my mortgage) went up in paranoia over the Mafia. Damn, damn.

The fight went as Angelo had expected. He was right. He was one out of 800 writers who believed Ali had a chance.

In the fourth round, Ali came back in the corner blinded. To this day, how this happened remains a mystery.

Let's look at it for the final time.

The foreign substance that Liston put in Ali's eye was what? The only *real* substance used to cauterize eye cuts was tincture of ferric chloride. It must be made fresh. By whom? A pharmacist. It's illegal, so why would any pharmacist make it? Moreover, if Liston, his manager, and his corner believed that Liston was going to knock Ali out in round one, why bother to make up a foreign substance to be given in round four? It doesn't make sense.

Liston in the third round started having shoulder problems. The corner then applied oil of wintergreen and rubbing alcohol. One tiny drop of this burns like hell. That drop converged in body sweat of Liston and landed in Ali's eye. Bingo!

I was at the foot of the ring stairs with Handsome Jimmy, Angie's older brother. I heard a Muslim torpedo say to the other guy, "Angelo has put stuff in his eyes. If he can't go on and quits the fight, we get Angelo right after the fight."

"Stick a knife in him," said the other one.

I quietly told Handsome Jimmy to tell Angelo to throw away the sponge—to get a new, clean sponge and use clear, new water to flush out the eyeball. This Angelo did, and as he saw the ref coming to see what was wrong, he shoved Ali out to face Liston, half blinded with the rubbing lotion. "Run, baby, run."

This Ali did. The eye cleared up, and Ali took Liston apart. Liston quit in the corner so he would have a chance for a rematch. The Mafia took a huge bath. So did Liston. They couldn't wait for the rematch.

As it turns out, it didn't do them any good.

Chris maintained a friendly but distant friendship, but Ali was very close to Angelo. He loved Angelo because Angelo was nonjudgmental; he pleased Ali in anything he wanted to do. Angelo was hopelessly in love with Ali. Ali represented his greatest dream, the perfect fighter. Angelo lived for the Ali fights. He would have worked for nothing. I did, but I had another method of making an income.

Once, at the beginning of the Muslim coup, Herbert refused to pay Angelo what he was worth or even what he was getting by contract. Angelo wanted to stay, but it was a humiliation. Angelo was worth every penny they ever paid him, but they humiliated him and made him sweat. Not that he wasn't well paid. But when one considers that in most fights Ali was making millions, Angelo's fee was microscopic. So was Sarria's. Why Ali didn't intervene was a part of the madness of the Ali Circus that I couldn't ever accept.

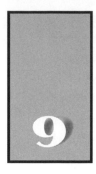

A Conversation with John Underwood

Notes Taken in a One-on-One Interview, April 18, 2004

John Underwood began writing for the old *Miami News* while still in high school, then moved on to the *Miami Herald* after earning a scholarship to the University of Miami. The *Herald* offered him a raise in salary and paid for half the scholarship. After service in the army and a stint as a feature writer on the *Herald* city desk, he moved on to *Sports Illustrated,* becoming senior writer. Despite virtually covering the world, he never lost his appreciation for Miami—and the 5th Street Gym.

John Underwood's Thoughts on the 5th Street Gym

"My first love was sports and I covered them all, but boxing seemed to me, in many respects, the most honest. In boxing, what you see between those ropes is what you get. Participants can't hide their defects.

"In due course I found myself spending a lot of time at the Fifth Street Gym. There I found that despite my youth I was treated as an equal; everybody in the gym seemed more than willing to talk. And without realizing it, I was conscripted into the 'University of Boxing' under professors Chris and Angelo Dundee. I learned despite myself, and it helped my writing because I was getting an inside look.

"In sports reporting there's only a fine line between editorial and plain news, and none allowed for a better chance to express yourself than boxing. Chris and Angelo made it easy. They were right out of [a] Damon Runyon [story], and they treated me as if I were Red Smith. They never stopped favoring me with their viewpoints."

One Underwood memory of that period was a fight Muhammad Ali (then still known as Cassius Clay) had with a very good light heavyweight named Doug Jones. Jones had been tough on heavyweights, and it was considered a risk when Angelo agreed to the match. It went off at virtually even money. Underwood covered it and, to his disappointment, thought he witnessed a sound beating of Clay.

"I had Jones winning eight rounds to Clay's two, but the decision went to Clay, unanimously. I was incredulous, and went to Chris afterward. 'How could they give Clay that fight?' I asked. 'Jones won at least eight rounds.'

"Chris's eyes crinkled in a smile behind those thick, black-frame glasses. He put his hand on my shoulder and whispered, 'It's not always a sweet science. Sometimes it's an *inexact science.*'"

Ferdie Interrupts with His Point of View

I could envision that. I could hear Chris's soft "heh, heh, heh," when he sent you off into the night to contemplate his wisdom.

Many, many years later I was searching for some way to keep Chris entertained. He had a massive stroke. He was incapacitated in a wheelchair and couldn't talk.

I came up with an idea. I invited some boxing experts to Chris's house to rack up a videotape of Cassius Clay versus Doug Jones. "Let's look at it today," I proposed. "Who really won that fight?" I had had it Clay by two.

Sitting around the set were the best minds in boxing: Hank Kaplan, ring historian; Ed Pope, *Miami Herald* sports editor; Murray Gaby, artist, boxer, CEO of the Mendoza group; and I. We pointedly did not invite Angelo, because he was obviously an Ali man. To him, Ali never lost. We knew Chris was a boxing man, though. He would see it fair and square.

Marty Kaplan (Murray Gaby) and Hank Kaplan (*right*) at the 5th Street Gym. Hank Kaplan Archive, Brooklyn College Library.

None saw it for Doug Jones—not even a draw. Ali won most of the rounds handily. What had happened? The writers and the public expected too much of Ali. In those days, he was undefeated and a KO puncher. Ali boxed Doug Jones to a decision, but the public wanted a KO.

When I reported this to Underwood, he was surprised. He thought the entire country had thought Doug Jones won it.

Underwood on Cassius Clay

Underwood laughed when he recalled the pleasure of covering the brash young Cassius Clay.

"He used to bring me his poetry, on little slips of paper, and if it wasn't exactly Keats, and had more than its share of grammatical ups and downs, it was always fun to read. He had a way with people. He called everybody by a nickname. After I moved to New York, I became *Sports Illustrated* and remained that way whenever our paths crossed."

Years later, Rocky Marciano invited Underwood to sit with him for the screening of the much-ballyhooed "computer fight" between Rocky and Ali. Marciano, long retired, lost weight, trained hard, and donned a toupee for the filming, which included what amounted to fifty rounds of scripted, faked fighting. Murray Woroner appointed a blue-ribbon panel to feed opinion into the computer, which vomited out, more or less, how the fight would go. Angelo knew Ali like a book. Chris knew Rocky Marciano. Murray then scripted the action punch by punch. They filmed thirteen different endings, adding to the suspense, and when it was finally shown on the air, Marciano was the winner.

When Underwood watched the final version with Marciano and his little group, he asked Rocky what, after spending all that time in the ring with him, he had learned about Ali.

"He shook his head as if amazed and said how quick Ali was, how fast his hands were, how well he snapped off his punches. Then he smiled and said, 'But I'da taken him. I'd have put him down. . . .'

"I believed him then, but I'm not so sure now. Too bad they weren't of the same era. It would have been a great fight. The regulars at the 5th Street Gym would still be talking about it."

10

When Ali Took On Marciano

The Fake Fight

Murray Woroner was a clever radio man who had a computerized script on the hour-by-hour birth of Christ. It played to a huge radio audience and won critical awards and financial rewards for him. Basking in the sunlight of critical acclaim, Murray looked for another project that would be suitable for turning into a computerized event.

It turned out that a spectacular possibility existed in Fort Lauderdale, under his very nose. It was big. It was important. And it was, at that moment, financially feasible.

Rocky Marciano had retired undefeated and lived in Fort Lauderdale. Rocky was barely forty, and he was stewing in his juices to come back. The boxing commission said no, no, no. Stay undefeated, a hero to your people, with a place in boxing history. Rocky hated his manager, and that kept him from attempting a comeback. Still, Rocky wanted to fight.

Ali found himself in a hard place during his exile of 1967–70 when, because of his opposition to the Vietnam War, he became a conscientious objector. The main problem was that he was forbidden to fight—not even an exhibition in Miami or anywhere in the known world. As soon as the Black Muslims realized that Ali could no longer produce funds for them and then realized that Ali expected them to finance his retirement, they threw him out of the church, forbade him to ever use his Muslim name, and barred every mosque from permitting him to pray there. Muhammad Ali was shut out by his own people. It was disgraceful.

But Muhammad is a resilient man. He hears what he wants to hear. He kept on calling himself Muhammad Ali, and he went to any mosque he pleased: who would turn him away? He devised ways to make enough money to survive on his own, without the Muslims.

Probably none was more bizarre and creative than the suggestion that Murray Woroner came up with, which was the possibility of matching two undefeated champions to fight in a computer fight, which was fully legal. Wow! What a feature!

Chris and Angelo leapt at the chance. Marciano's people were tap dancing with joy. When he heard the story, Marciano began to diet and workout and ordered a new toupee.

The Muslims were furious, for they had cut themselves out of the loop. They were outside looking in, and their cash cow was ready to produce income for Murray Woroner but none for the Honorable Elijah Muhammad.

Murray was a genius in organizing the writing. He got himself a blue-ribbon panel of boxing experts, writers, fight people, and ex-boxers. They each submitted ideas on how a round would go, and Murray collated all the data through a master computer located in Birmingham, Alabama. This produced a shooting script, and they moved into a small movie studio for the filming. It would be a movie to be seen in theaters.

Angelo worked Ali's corner. Marciano had a friend, Mel Zeigler, help in his corner. He wanted no one known in boxing, at least, to carry his towel, spit bucket, and stool. But Marciano wouldn't need a known corner man. After all, it was a scripted film.

Rocky Marciano was a plain, wonderful, northern sort of Italian, with apparently hundreds of friends. He couldn't turn anyone down, except for money; Rocky was a cheapskate and hoarder of pennies. In fact, that was what caused his death. He was up north in Chicago. A friend called, asking Rocky to come to a relative's birthday party. He had a private plane and would pay $200 in cash. Rocky needed only to appear, shake a few hands, and catch a plane back to Florida, where his wife and child awaited. The plane crashed in a rainstorm in Newton, Iowa, and hit a tree; Rocky died. What a shame, for a measly $200.

Rocky had a love-hate thing going with Ali. He was convinced that in his prime, he would have beaten Ali. He just couldn't give Ali the credit the younger man deserved. He didn't think Ali was tough enough to stand up to the body blows of Marciano. Rocky had good reason for his high opinion of himself: he was undefeated at 49–0 (with 43 KO's). Even the great Joe Louis had caved in to his dreadful attack, and so had Archie Moore.

Rocky's main problem in boxing was not with opponents, it was his undying hatred of his manager, Al Weill. Weill was one of those detestable managers who thrived on denigrating his fighters by telling the press how dumb the boxer was, how he couldn't think for himself, and how he needed a keeper. Most of the time, he refused to call Rocky by name and used the old manager's moniker, "Fighter." And when referring to the fighter and the camp, it always came out "I." "I knocked out Archie Moore. I'm fighting Ezzard Charles." It was funny to the press. It wasn't funny to Marciano. Weill also cut in for a large percentage of the purse.

As Marciano grew into a top attraction and boxing men reluctantly conceded that Rocky Marciano was the greatest boxer in the world, Weill escalated his own fame and position.

The end came when Weill had the incredible chutzpah to actually slap Marciano in front of a full press conference. It was all Rocky could do not to knock Weill silly. Cooler heads prevailed, but Weill was out and Rocky, tied up by contracts while also hampered by a bad back, had no choice but to retire. His exit was applauded by his wife and daughter.

Many times during Sonny Liston's reign, Rocky, chafing at the bit and still a young man, wanted to come out of retirement, but the thought of making a dollar for Weill and his wife's insistence that he stay retired kept him at home.

While Rocky and the boxing world thought the huge, hard-punching Sonny Liston might be a stretch for the retired and flabby Marciano, no such caution was exhibited when Cassius Clay was mentioned. Men and boys. Then when Sonny was TKO'd by Muhammad Ali, Rocky saw red. He was sure that he could come out of retirement, train hard, and steamroll the kid. The thought of Weill benefiting kept Rocky at bay, though his restraint was killing him. He was sure that he could roll over Ali.

As far as Ali was concerned, he never studied opponents or fretted about who he was going to fight next. His philosophy, born of supreme self-confidence, was simply, "Bring 'em on. Whoever he is, I'll knock him out."

Ali never gave Rocky Marciano a thought as a possible opponent, because Marciano simply was not available. Why worry about an aging champion tied up in a bitter dispute with his manager and with a wife who wouldn't even consider a comeback? Rocky Marciano was simply not a consideration in his plans.

When he signed on for the computer fight, Ali was amused by the thought that people were around who still thought Rocky had a chance with him. "Even in his prime, Rocky had no chance with me. First thing, he is too little. Less than five foot ten to my six foot three inches. I'd overwhelm him, I'd lay on him in the clinches like a big old grizzly bear, and I'd smother his insides out. He was too small to reach me from outside. I'd jab him twenty to one. Rocky had a face that cut easily. Can you imagine what my stinging jab would do to those weak eyes? By round three, Rocky would look like he ran into a lawn mower. How could he beat me? No way, is how."

This was before three Frazier fights, three fights with Ken Norton, and the George Foreman fight proved Ali's hypothesis. Ali too big, Ali too fast, Ali too strong a puncher, Ali too fast a jab, and the bad news, Ali too tough, takes heavy punishment well. In the light of what we saw during his long career, I'm afraid Ali was right. Marciano, while a formidable opponent, wouldn't have lasted long.

Oh, I know. Every time I speak at the Sons of Italy banquets, I get hooted down.

"Look what Rocky done to Ali in that fight they had! He beat Ali," they would yell in my face.

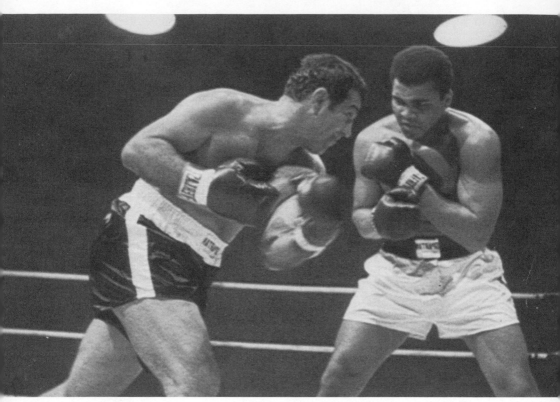

Marciano *(left)* trying to avoid a left jab by Ali.

"Well, yes and no. In your city, Rocky won. In Ali's city, Chicago, Louisville, et cetera, Ali won. In some it was a draw. In some Rocky lost on a cut, et cetera.

"Fellers, it was a filmed fight, a fake. They wrote it. It was a scripted fight. They needed fifteen rounds. They wrote fifteen rounds."

I'm amazed by the public perception of that fight. I watched it in the Miami Beach Auditorium along with Chris and Angelo. People rushed to me after the fight. The press put microphones in my face:

"How bad was the cut?"

"How many stitches did it take to stop it?"

"When can he fight again?"

"Did the cut retire Rocky again?"

"Fellers, it was a fake fight," I had to say. "It was a scripted fight filmed in a studio with no audience. The cut was fake with fake blood, do you understand? Like actors in a movie."

No one listened. Boy, what a job we did with that fight.

But they wouldn't listen. That's what they saw with their own eyes, and their thinking went like this: "I don't care what anyone says, Rocky got cut real bad. And the only reason he lost was the cut."

Even today, people persist in feeling that the fight was real. While writing this book, I spoke to several expert sportswriters who argued violently that Marciano had beaten Ali in a fifteen-round decision. They refused to believe that Ali won in Ali-land.

"Yeah, in Miami, you're right. In Chicago it was Ali. In most of Europe, except of course Italy, it was Ali."

They seemed mortified that they were cheated, flimflammed. "Fix," they wanted to scream. "But it's a movie," we would answer. Years later, the Black Muslims decided they needed a biography about Ali. They sent Ali with Richard Durham (who, in Ali's camp, was known as "Hemingway") to interview Murray Woroner. Woroner refused to see him, for not only had he spent his profits trying to get the then-banned Ali a title fight, but also he was getting flogged in the black press by favoring Marciano. They saw it as a racist trick.

Ali asked me to arrange an interview at Murray's house. I assured Murray that it would be fine; they were just writing the story of the computerized fight with Marciano. Murray's wife, who had responded badly to the racist slurs they were receiving, had to be cooled off.

As we approached the pool, Ali whispered to me, "Stay out of this, Doc, we don't want your name in this." Uh-oh. I could see that Durham had come loaded for bear. He whipped out a tape recorder and had twenty racist questions for the amazed Woroner, such as this:

"Where was the computer used to write the script?"

"Birmingham."

"That's in Alabama?" Durham narrowed his eyes and looked conspiratorially at Ali. "In the South. How many white guys on the board of experts?" Durham asked.

"About fifty-fifty. We had big names like Sugar Ray Robinson, Joe Louis, and those guys." Murray started getting the drift that they were there to sandbag him.

This was the height of chutzpah. Murray Woroner was a very liberal man who had supported black causes during the days of segregation.

Although he forbade his children to use the "n- word" in his house, here were Ali and Durham screaming it at every turn. It was downright embarrassing to be there. Soon Murray finished the interview in which he had been reviled and accused of blatant racism. His wife was livid. I had my head down.

Nonplussed, Ali put his arm around Murray as we walked to the car.

"Say, bossman," said Ali, turning Uncle Tom before our disbelieving eyes, "you think you can advance me two hundred dollars out of your advances?"

"I don't carry that kind of money in my bathing suit," said Murray through clenched teeth.

"Ask your wife," said Ali innocently.

"I don't think so," I said, taking him by the arm and putting him in my car.

"This is the kind of stuff we need," said Durham happily.

The injustice of that horrible afternoon was that Ali had benefited the most from the computer fight. It kept his name alive. It showed him boxing again. It made him a nice sum of money right at the time that he was down with nobody showing up to lend him a helping hand. It brought Ali to the front again as an employable name. Campus dates and speaking dates followed. Murray Woroner's wonderful idea had legitimized Ali as a commodity once again and saved his financial life. It was a huge plus!

Murray Woroner took the interview very hard, for he, like all who came under Ali's spell, had come to believe that he was somehow part of Ali's inside family. He wasn't, he couldn't be, for he was white.

Not long after, Murray Woroner had his last heart attack and died. Soon after, so did his wife.

What had started out as a joyful, fun-filled event to help out Ali turned into a sad major tragedy.

What a shame.

As to the filming of the fight, it was enjoyable and basically uneventful. Three 8–hour days, in and out; it was easy.

Regardless of the script, Rocky seemed unable to pull his punches, whereas Ali could come within a fraction of an inch to making it look

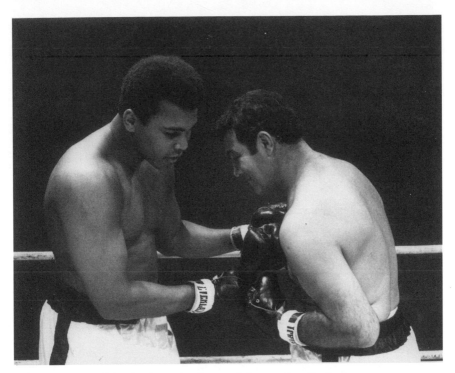

Ali on the ropes while Marciano simulates a right punch to the body.

extremely real. Our problem was that Ali was getting madder and madder as Rocky thumped one hard shot after another off his ribs.

By the end of the second day, Ali stopped the filming to have a word with Rocky.

"Rocky, you're supposed to be pulling those body shots. You aren't, and they're hurting my ribs. Now, if we're going to have a real fight, then you will not be able to land those shots without me peppering your face with hard left jabs and right hooks, and if you do by chance land a body shot, you're going to take back a stinging right hand to the nose to break it again. Now, do we play movie or do we play boxing?"

By the last three rounds, they quit trying to pull their punches and let fly. Watch those rounds closely. That's more like it would have been. That alone was worth money.

Marciano knew he was wrong. Secretly, he wanted to find out if Ali could take his best body shots. To his surprise, he found that Ali could. End of the problem.

ALI MEETS MARCIANO IN COMPUTER FIGHT miami

pacheco

CHRIS DUNDEE REFEREE

I had a lot of fun showing a round or two when I went on a speaking tour. A curious thing happened. I would show a couple of rounds of the first or second Ali-Liston fight and then the filmed fight. Without exception, the audience always got excited about the fake fight and wanted to see more. The real fight wasn't as exciting.

I found that a nice justification for the job Murray Woroner did in writing, staging, and shooting the two undefeated champions in a steamy little studio in South Miami.

Too bad Murray did not get the credit due to him or the money he should have made with proper distribution.

If you don't take away anything else from this chapter, let me reiterate. Commit this to memory.

1. It was a movie that followed a script.
2. There were thirteen endings, depending on where it was shown.
3. The cut was bogus.
4. Ali would have beaten Marciano if they had ever really fought.

The R. J. Reynolds and Al Jones Saga

A lovable giant, Al Jones was the stuff that boxing managers' dreams are made of. Chris Dundee almost fainted when Al Jones walked into the 5th Street Gym.

Alan Jones was six feet six inches tall and was muscular perfection on a huge scale. He had come of his own accord. He wanted to fight for the heavyweight championship of the world.

There was one hitch. He was sweet natured. There was not one spark of aggression in his huge body. He was a walking personification of Ferdinand the Bull. You can't teach a pacifist to be mean. No matter what you did, Al Jones smiled.

Chris Dundee could motivate any of the Twelve Apostles to be a killer. He got Angelo Dundee to teach Al Jones about the moves and Lou Gross to "bird dog" him to keep him innocent. That proved to be no problem, because Al was a mama's boy. He volunteered to work with underprivileged kids. He was a wonder of "do a good deed," and he was kind to all.

Chris, the master of match making, wisely picked a series of opponents. The Dundee Golden Rule was this: Match him with fighters who could give him a fight and who could present a danger. Not a fight, a "danger" of a fight.

Soon, the Dundees had another heavyweight in position to challenge for the title, which, by the way, they owned. Al Jones was undefeated in nine fights. He looked like a sure thing.

When Chris felt that Al was ready for moving up to contention, he made his choice of opponent. He chose a tough nut named Jerry Quarry. The 5th Street Gym was aflutter with excitement. The gym filled to see Big Al work out. Patiently he signed autographs. Nothing seemed to impress him. Fame and celebrity did not affect him.

Jerry Quarry was a very tough kid. He was white and tough as nails. Ali had beaten him twice. Jimmy Ellis had out-pointed him for the title, and Joe Frazier had beaten him to a pulp in New York. He was tough as hell but beatable.

Still, he was a top-dollar attraction because, although he had lost to the best, he had beaten the rest.

Quarry came from a corrupt, acrimonious top driver of Irish street fighters, the meanest of whom was his father, who was prone to punching his kids in the corner if they weren't doing well. Sometimes the fights in the corner were better than the ones going on inside the ropes.

I shuddered to think of all of that violence going up against the amicable face of Al Jones. I envisioned that peaceful mass of humanity going down, a serene smile on his face.

Then, on Sunday, as the fight neared, fate interfered and Al Jones was relieved from his task. As Jones drove his car down a country road going to do his predawn run, a farmer's truck slammed into his car.

Al Jones wasn't badly hurt, but his hand was. It was fractured in various places. The injury was serious. Not only was the Quarry fight history, but also no one knew whether he would ever fight again.

Chris was beside himself. To make matters worse, Ed Pope had called me and got the real story. Al Jones had sustained a bad hand fracture. The Tuesday fight was off. The story ran in the Monday *Herald*.

This sent Chris Dundee into orbit. He called Pope in a rage.

"Who said the fight was off?" Chris screamed.

"Is it off or on?" Pope asked in confusion.

"It's off, but couldn't you hold off printing that until it was Tuesday?"

"But, Chris, we are newspaper people, not your partner. We print the truth."

"Who are you, George Washington?" Chris screamed into the red phone. At a loss as to how to answer that, Ed Pope hung up. Chris stayed sore at Pope for a year. Pope didn't notice.

Six months of therapy did not help the fracture. The hand was so badly fractured that I called in my friend, plastic surgeon Dr. Howard Gordon, a specialist in hand fracture. He had to put four rods in Jones's gigantic hand.

It was touch and go as to whether he would ever fight again. Al Jones was a quiet, wonderful patient. Chris got him the best liability lawyer on Miami Beach.

Jay Swidler was an ace in the courtroom because he shared the same sweet demeanor as his client. He was thirty-five but looked twenty-five. He wore perfectly tailored suits that were carefully pressed, and his shoes were always shined. He spoke softly with a slight southern accent and a big smile. He always seemed to be hearing some inside joke in his head. He'd been a local football hero, and women loved him; he represented the kind of man parents hoped their daughter would bring home.

Day after day, watching these two kind-faced, amiable men sitting side by side working magic on the adoring jury, I was feeling sorry for the insurance company. Every day Chris raised the jury award in his head, and the figures danced up to half a million. Swidler questioned his main medical witness: me. "Doctor, do you think Big Al will ever fight again?"

"No, sir, he'll never fight again."

Al looked down with a blank expression.

"I now call Doctor Howard Gordon, a hand surgeon who inserted the four pins that are in his hand today." Swidler questioned him: "Doctor, based on your vast experience with fighters, do you think that Big Al will ever fight again?"

Gordon: "No, sir. It's as bad a facture as I have ever seen. He will never fight again."

Al Jones looked at his hand with a blank, almost disinterested expression.

Swidler: "You've been his doctor since he first stepped into the 5th Street Gym, and you know him well."

Me: "Yes, sir, he has a perfect body."

"And in your opinion, will he ever be able to fight?"

Me: "Not in his lifetime."

Big Al did not look at me, as he stared at his hand.

"I would now like to call Chris Dundee, the foremost sports figure and promoter in the country." Swidler asked him, "First of all, what did the fight mean to Al Jones—a million dollars?"

Chris: "First, a half million dollars in the Quarry fight. Then he was in line for a million-dollar shot if he won the title. Close to fifty million would be possible."

Swidler: "So this injury has cost Jones possibly millions in income."

The opposing attorney looked as if he had taken a series of hard body shots. He couldn't stay quiet. Although he was out of order and knew it, still he had to break the spell being cast over the jury by expert testimony. Not able to contain himself, the opposing attorney yelled at Chris.

"Yes! That's if he beat Jerry Quarry. What if Al Jones lost? How much would he be worth then?"

The judge banged the gavel, but Chris knew how to work a jury, too. Quickly he answered, "But first off, he knocks out Jerry Quarry in five rounds. Mortal cinch. If by some reason Jones loses to Jerry Quarry, then Jones would only be worth fifty thousand dollars at the worst."

The defense attorney looked like he had been shot in the heart.

"Sit down and shut up. We are getting killed here. If they get in a few more shots like that here, the judge might give you the chair," said the insurance company guy.

"At this time, I would like to introduce his manager, Angelo Dundee, manager of seventeen champions, including Muhammad Ali." Swidler said.

Angelo: "Since his first fight, since he first set foot in the 5th Street Gym, I've never seen a fighter that looked more like Ali."

Swidler: "I imagine you were sad to hear he had destroyed his right hand."

Angelo: "Crushed. Devastated. He is like a son to me."

Swidler: "Is it just possible that he might fight again, that he could come back?"

"No. Not possible. And if he tried to come back I wouldn't let him." Angelo looked pityingly at Big Al.

The room was silent Al Jones was history. He shifted his weight in his chair and never took his eyes away from his hands.

They broke for lunch. Swidler and his gang were going to his office to celebrate. The defense then repaired to choose a church to do the stations of the cross.

The time had come; the bomb was ready to drop. Hiroshima again. Al Jones took the stand. His huge 6'6" frame dropped into the chair. Swidler decided to understate the case, as he felt that doing anything more would be overkill, repetitive, and unnecessary. He waited for a long minute, then dramatically placed his hand on Al Jones's hand and spoke slowly and succinctly.

"Al, you've heard the world-famous fight doctor Doctor Ferdie Pacheco, your manager-trainer, Angelo Dundee, and the famous and experienced promoter Chris Dundee testify under oath that you will never fight again. Never compete in the ring, never have a chance to compete for the title, never win the title.

"What do you say to that, Al?"

The jurors leaned forward, their hearts breaking.

For the first time, Jones looked up and said in a strong, clear voice, "I don't care what they all says, I said I want to keep on fighting." The sound in the crowded courtroom was the bloody yell of Chris Dundee.

Counsel for defense: defense rests.

Except for one last shot, Al Jones would never make money for Chris or Angelo again. His settlement out of court was $30,000.

R. J. Reynolds and Al Jones

There is very little difference (that I can see) between the denizens of that adult playpen up the coast a bit, Palm Beach, with its collection of indolent, wealthy trust-fund millionaires, and the better-off Miami

Beach millionaires. They are both sort of worthless people. They have nothing to occupy them all week long, so they do hard drugs, smoke crack, and drink up a storm, and they try to fill in the blank spaces in between.

This gives them too much time to fill, so they try to find sports hobbies such as getting into horse racing, car racing, speedboat racing—all very expensive. And from time to time, one of them falls for boxing. It is exciting but cheap as expensive hobbies go. But the allure is undeniable.

I drew the attention of a tall, pulpy, handsome young man, a few years younger than me. He loved boxing. He followed me to fights. He was at the gym all the time. He had been a boxer at Harvard and still liked to work out. Everybody liked him. No one knew that he was R. J. Reynolds III, scion of the Reynolds tobacco company.

R.J. was a very nice, sweet man. He was virtually a kind of simpleton. He gave away his money, and in truth he needed a keeper. One day at the Daytona Dog Track, he met his "keeper." The girl was the daughter of a rough-and-tumble racetrack tout, horse handicapper, card shark, big-time gambler, and pimp. He had brought up his daughter by his side. She was wiry, thin, and athletic. She was a tough tomboy. Marie should have been born a boy, but she wasn't. It's not that she was born facially good looking; truth is, she looked like Sea Biscuit.

Well, she took over the hapless R.J. and ran him to death. R.J. (whom she called Josh) became her slave.

One night, when R.J. was bitten by the boxing bug, he decided that he would like to invest about $12,000 to buy a piece of a huge, undefeated black kid, Al Jones. Al was six feet six inches of pure punching power. He had KO'd everyone in sight. Chris was ready to move him up the ladder. Jerry Quarry sounded about right.

Marie, never the one to loosen the reins of leadership, insisted on going to see Al Jones to evaluate him and decide whether *she* wanted to invest $12,000 on Al.

I sat with Marie at ringside. After three rounds of evaluating Al Jones's devastating power, Marie spoke.

Al Jones *(left)* and Luis Sarria. Bob East/*Miami Herald*.

"He can be hit by a straight right hand. I'll bet you Josh can get in there and hit Al Jones with a right hand all night long."

I told her, "You are so full of shit, Marie." (She was like a "guy" from being around stables all her life and talked salty herself.)

"I'm thinking of investing twelve thousand dollars on Jones," she reminded me. "I'll make a bet, if Josh can hit him with straight rights, I *won't* buy him. If he can't hit him, I'll put up the twelve thousand that same day."

Josh said, "She's kidding, Doc. I haven't boxed for ten years."

Marie replied, "No, I'm not. You'll train for two weeks. After all, it's only three two-minute rounds and he won't punch you. So, OK? Deal?"

"In two weeks, on Sunday, noon," I replied. "It's a deal, pending Angelo's okay. He is the boss."

Marie could read Josh like a book, but every once in a while she badly misread him. Down deep inside the acquiescent victim facade of the henpecked, R.J. stood his ground and yelled, "No, I won't." He was very scared of Marie and usually putty in her hands. So he rebelled in his way, and in this case his way consisted of disappearing into the black ghetto bars and getting falling-down drunk, then getting beaten up, robbed, and taken home by the whore of the night. He disappeared. It was his way of saying no.

Bar of Palm Bay Club—Marie Talks to Ferdie

"He's been gone for the entire week. I'm worried now. He ain't never been gone longer than a week before."

"That was your mistake," I said. "You gave him two weeks to train. Well, he's got one more week to go. Relax. They love him in the ghetto. He has his regular lost weekend buddies and bartenders who protect him. And I got Holston's boys sticking to him like glue. They'll bring him back the Saturday before the fight."

"What shape will he be in with all that drinking?" she asked.

"He's in great shape to take a beating. Every night he gets at least one beating before he goes to bed. He's used to a beating!"

Sunday Noon: 5th Street Gym

The place is unusually quiet. In front of his locker is Willie Johnson, the sparring partner, who works with Al Jones and is wrapping his own hands. A few stalls away, Angelo is wrapping Al's hands. We await the appearance of Josh Reynolds. Nobody, least of all Doc, believes he'll show. Doc has brought Kleinberg to write up the "fight," but he doesn't believe it either.

Ferdie: "Do you know who R. J. Reynolds III is?"

Willie: "Naw. A building?"

Ferdie: "He's one of the richest men in America. And he's coming to do three rounds with Al Jones."

Willie: "You mean if Al slaps that turkey upside the head and a hundred-dollar bill falls to the floor, I kin pick it up and keep it?"

Ferdie: "Yeah, something like that."

Kleinberg: "He ain't gonna show. I might as well do a story on Chip Johnson. I hear he is the first boxer to turn Black Muslim. Now *that* is a story. You seen him, Willie?"

Willie: "You mean has I seen Harold 23 X Hashid? Yeah. Yesterday the cops stopped him on the stairs 'cause he was carrying a bag with his stuff."

Howard: "What'd they find? What was in the bag?"

Willie: "Oh, they found three pork chops, a package of cigarettes, three miniatures of Jack Daniel's, and that address of a white woman."

Howard: "And . . . so?"

Willie: "Well, they arrested him for impersonating a Muslim, and he's over in jail."

At this moment, Josh appears at the door with a worried-looking Marie. Josh looks predictably awful. He is bloated, and his skin is a mottled light green color with black and blue bruises all over his body.

Ferdie: "Where is his equipment?"

Marie: "He ain't got no boxing gear. I thought you'd rent us some. We'll *pay*."

Ferdie: "Marie, this ain't no stable renting horses."

Willie: "I'll rent him mine, all of it."

Josh takes a good bleary-eyed look at the imposing figure of Al Jones, 6'6", in street clothes.

With a minimum of small talk, they get into the ring, Angelo with Al in the corner, Ferdie with poor Josh. Marie has the balls to get into the ring to second Josh. I throw her out. She is not happy. She would be happy if *she* were going to fight Al Jones.

Angelo: "Now, don't throw no real punches. This sucker has twelve thousand dollars he's dying to give us. Just do *not* let one right hand hit you. And—just a reminder—don't hurt him!"

R. J. Reynolds III. Bob East/*Miami Herald*.

Al Jones (mock angry face): "Right! Right! Right! I'm going to kill the white motherfucker the first good punch I hit him with."

Bang! The bell.

Angie (weakly): "No, don't."

Al does his job well. He moves around with excellent footwork while Josh throws slow, clumsy punches—all of which miss by a mile. Al doesn't throw a real punch, but to keep it real he tip-taps a light punch to the headgear without effect. Then Al throws a left hook to the body, not hard but with a little sting. Josh turns purple and goes over to his corner and throws up a bucket of Gatorade.

Howard: "There goes Friday and Saturday night."

Ferdie: "One more round, please God."

The rounds are complete. Josh has survived. All the boxers good-naturedly pat him on the back. Marie is hurriedly stripping Josh. No right has landed. But where is the $12,000?

Marie: "I'll see you tomorrow, Angelo."

Josh: "I want to keep Willie's equipment as a souvenir—and proof that I went three hard rounds with Al Jones."

Willie: "That'll be two hundred dollars, including my favorite shoes."

Marie (peels off two one-hundred-dollar bills): "Fair enough, Willie."

Josh: "Give Willie one more. He's a good man."

Looking down the stairs from the dark of the gym, to the bright lights of the Miami sun-drenched street, I see Josh being half carried down the stairs, with Marie on one side and Willie Johnson on the other.

Ferdie: "You think you'll ever see the twelve thousand dollars?"

Angie: "What do you think?"

Supper with Chris Dundee
(and Willie Pastrano)

"Doc, whatcha doing for dinner?"

The voice of Chris always made me happy. "Nothing."

"Good. Pick you up at five."

"Five. Christ, it's four forty-five now."

"It gives you time to shower and shave. Wear something cool. Like a white guayabera."

Something cool? Uh-oh, I thought. What was I getting into?

Before I could figure out the double talk he was giving me, I was on a runway and on one of those little antique amphibian planes going to one of the islands. So far, there was no supper in sight.

"Did you bring your bag?" he asked, as we were landing on the beautiful sparkling bay of an unknown island.

"My bag? Since when do I bring medical tools to eat supper?"

"I don't know. You're a doctor, ain'cha?" He gave me an accusing fish-eye stare. "Aren't you always prepared for emergencies?"

"I guess it slipped my mind," I said lamely.

We barely made it to the fight. We were there to do an exhibition bout for Willie Pastrano, who was then the light heavyweight champion. From the look of Willie, nobody had told him of the fight ahead of time either. He groaned and crawled into a cot to sleep for a few more

Chris Dundee *(right)* and Ferdie in the 5th Street Gym. Lynn Pelham.

hours. The natives spread the mosquito netting over Willie and managed to catch a few squadrons of mosquitoes inside the netting. Sweet dreams, Willie.

The "arena" turned out to be a big clearing in the jungle. Big planks placed on tree trunks were the seats. The ring was an elevated square of the planks covered by canvas. The ropes were three garden hoses nailed to the corners, formed by pylons. For stools, we had kitchen chairs. For lights, we had overturned water buckets with a pair of 150–watt lights inside. There were four of those. They didn't provide much light but appeared to give a great comfort to thousands of black mosquitoes. For a bell, we had a bell from an old shipwrecked schooner. When it sounded, you could have heard it all the way back to Miami. Willie had given the ring a cursory glance as he walked by on the way to his cot.

"Christ, Chris. I have to fight in there?"

"What fight? You'll knock the chump out in one round and we'll go home."

Chris was greeted like a movie star by the Bahamian commission. Chris carefully politicized each and every one, engaging them by so-

liciting their opinion on the upcoming Jerry Quarry versus Al Jones fight.

"Who do you think will win? Quarry or Al Jones?" Each one puffed up in importance as he got a chance to tell the king of boxing his opinion. They didn't know that Chris would ask everyone he met—from the airplane pilot to stewardesses to custom agents—what they thought of his big fight.

The crowd was there early, as they seldom got to see a real champion box this far back in the boonies. The rest of the card was comprised of "homies": Bahamians with scant experience against the very dregs of the 5th Street Gym.

The crowd grew impatient. Chris took me by the arm to the dressing rooms.

"Hurry up, Doc!" he said in his agitated Kermit the Frog manner.

"What?" I hadn't heard that I had to do anything.

"Examine the first fighters."

"Examine them with what? I didn't bring my bag."

He handed me a soup spoon. "You know, look in his throat, look in his ear. Can he hear you? Does he talk? Can he see it? OK so he can fight."

I started the first exam.

"Then wrap their hands," Chris said.

"The entire undercard? Plus Willie?" I asked. That would mean twelve hand wrappings in all.

"Well, they can't fight without it," he said with a certain amount of logic.

It took forever. In the meantime, the 5th Street Gym pro fighters were knocking out the amateur fighters as quickly as I could wrap them. Willie smiled as each boxer came back. "Piece of cake!" said one of our guys. "These guys can't fight even a little bit."

Willie gleamed. "Call me when it's five minutes to fight time." Willie turned over and went back to sleep wrapped in a mosquito net.

I'd finished and sat down exhausted. I was not only a forty-five-year-old doctor but also one badly out of shape. I felt tired and abused by raging mosquitoes that found my skin an inviting target.

"You're through?" Chris came back rubbing his hands. "We need you to work the corner. Take the spit bucket. The black kid is all alone out there!"

"Chris, they're all black," I said.

I wondered if this was the way Angelo started. It's enough to say that, that night, I didn't personally know one fighter I worked with, much less his name, much less his talent.

Chris had saved the fight before Pastrano to last a bit more than one round. These boys were not good, but they were tough. The kid lasted to the fifth round, and I found myself exhausted but working the corner.

One boy, breathing hard as he waited to answer the bell for the fifth round, leaned back and asked me, "Can you do something about the mosquitoes? If they keep on biting me, I'm going to go down."

"Good idea," I said, imagining the official scoring TKO, 5, because of mosquito bites.

I came back after my ordeal to find Pastrano glistening with oil of citronella smeared over him. "Good idea. That'll last about one round, Willie. Try to KO this guy in one!"

"I heard that," said Willie, inserting his mouthpiece.

Chris came in with a striped shirt for a referee. "What size are you, medium or large?"

"Large," I said, with a sinking feeling. "Why?"

"You're refereeing the Pastrano fight!"

"Chris, I'm a doctor. I've never refereed a bout."

"Can you count to ten?" I nodded. "Well?" Case closed. I put on the shirt. Willie went in and the crowd went wild.

Chris pulled me over as I went up the ring stairs. "Announce the fighters."

"Who, me?"

Chris gave me a look of disdain. "You can speak English, can't you?" Damn, Chris had an answer for everything.

I guess you can say that my announcing started on this night. It was well received. I liked it.

"Don't forget to tell them about the Big Al Jones and Jerry Quarry on March twenty-fifth in Miami."

"Go away, Chris. For God's sake, leave me alone."

The fight started. Of course, Willie looked like a million bucks. But the heavyset Bahamian took all his punches and seemed to enjoy the round. He smiled blissfully as punch after punch rained on his face.

"Who the fuck is this guy? He took my hardest left-hand uppercut and smiled like I just fed him a bonbon," said Willie.

"Bear down, Willie, it's hot as hell," I said in the corner.

"Oh, I haven't noticed," said Willie, heavy with sarcasm.

For the first time, I felt total exhaustion. The ring lights, blazing down on us, had squadrons of mosquito dive-bombers circling around in a black cloud.

By round five, Willie's mouth was wide open. He was swallowing as much water as he could get down. His eyes were getting blank.

"Can I lose my title if I quit?" asked Willie.

"Who knows? Chris is so diabolical that he might have arranged it that way so we could have a big bucks rematch in Miami," I said dejectedly.

The bell sounded for round six. I have to admit, in all my years of working fights, I never paid attention to the referee. If the ref is good, like Mills Lane, you never notice him. What you would never expect is what heavy work it is. I never thought a ref could get tired. I was reeling.

Willie began clinching as much as he could and as long as he could, and Willie was talking, talking, talking to his fat Bahamian opponent.

"Go down, man. I don't want to hit you no more. It's OK, you've fought a brave fight. Go down."

"No, champ, you ain't hurt me none. I smoked three joints before I came in here. Your punches feel good. I'm used to the heat. You just punch as you like."

Willie looked at me with that "Do something!" look. I was thinking of disqualifying the guy, but the guy did nothing but take punches, which each round were getting weaker and weaker. The crowd was into it now!

To make it worse, in round four, Chris had come by and said, "I hope you're keeping score. You're the only scorer."

"In an exhibition?"

"Yeah, you know who wins. It's like wrestling."

Oh, boy. Heat, mosquitoes, exhaustion, and now a hostile crowd to face. Wait till they hear that Pastrano won!

In round eight, Willie said to me, "Disqualify the guy."

"For what, Willie?"

"Fighting," he said with a straight face.

By round nine, Willie was on shaky legs. His back was covered with red welts from the mosquitoes. He walked to where I stood in the neutral corner.

"Who do you have to fuck to get out of here?"

"Chris Dundee," I said and signaled for the bell to ring.

I did notice that Chris had taken over the timekeeping duties. Rounds were now significantly shorter. Round eight had been a 2–minute round. I was sure round nine would be 1½ minutes, and God save us, round ten might even be just 1 minute.

The fat guy was still grinning from ear to ear.

"I wish I'd have smoked some of the grass this guy did before he got in here," said Willie, who had fought stoned a number of times.

Round ten came. Willie made up his mind to last a minute and quit.

Chris Dundee. Luisita Sevilla Pacheco.

Chris knew Willie very well, for he rang the bell at one minute. The crowd went wild. Apparently the betting action was that the native would last ten rounds with Willie. Not win. Just last.

I elected to simplify things and avoid bloodshed (mine) by saying, "The winner and still champion, Willie Pastrano!"

There was no use holding up his arm. His corner men were carrying him to the dressing room, where Willie quickly dressed and split for the hotel and a cold shower.

I was whipped. I'd never been so tired.

Chris came to get me before he went to the box office to "settle up."

"Meet you in the car." I got up on unsteady feet.

"What car? You got to call a taxi."

"Chris, it's twenty miles back to the town."

"So what? It comes off the top. Come on, let's go down and settle."

I dreaded this, for I knew how Chris dealt with figures and how he short-counted fighters, officials, and the promoter.

It was quicker than I expected. I sat by Chris and a heap of money.

"Fighter Louis gets nine dollars and fifty cents. Count it out, Doc."

"Me? What am I, an accountant?"

"You're a college graduate, ain'cha?"

"What's the fifty cents for?" asked the boxer.

"We gave you a Coke after the fight," said Chris. "Next. Abraham gets eight seventy-five. Count it, Doc."

So it went. The 5th Street Gym fighters would be paid in Miami on Monday.

The poor promoter waiting and hoping he wouldn't get robbed looked at the pathetic profits of the infernal night: $16.50.

"What?" he managed to say.

"Posters. We put up a lot of posters."

"I didn't see any," the man said simply.

"Not here. In Miami, all over the joint. Did you see them?"

"No. I live here, not Miami."

"Well, that's why you didn't see them."

Chris folded a fat roll around his rubber band and put it in his special pocket just as a dilapidated cab came by. We leapt in and vanished.

The night seemed to get even hotter. Swarms of mosquitoes came in through the front windows, stopped to bite us, and flew out the back.

The jungle was pitch black. We were on a narrow road with a ditch on each side. The driving was iffy because the driver kept gulping from a Ron Rico bottle.

"Say, driver." Chris tapped him hard on the shoulder. "How do you think big Al Jones is going to do against Jerry Quarry? I got the fight March twenty-fifth in Miami Beach."

The driver took a huge slug. Here he was a nobody and this hot-shot promoter wanted his advice! He thought it out carefully, turned around, put his right arm over the front seat, and with the other hand gesticulating wildly while letting go of the steering wheel, said, "The way I see it—"

At that point, the cab went ass over teakettle. We rolled over twice and ended up upside-down in the roadside ditch.

There was a moment of silence and then Chris asked (as we hung suspended with our heads up against the top of the back seat), "Which side . . . ? Did he say? Quarry or Jones?"

The Rise and Fall of the Mendoza Group

Murray Gaby had everything he could desire: professional success, a lovely family, creative satisfaction. He was happily married to a stunning clotheshorse model, Julie, and they had a talented wonderful daughter named Stacy, whom he adored. His ad agency was considered one of the best in South Florida; his six-figure income was considered the best in the ad business. In addition to professional success, Murray was considered one of the top painters and sculptors in Miami. And in a midlife crisis, with all that success, he determined that he should learn to play piano. This he also did. What, then, was lacking? At a midlife crisis, Murray returned to his first love, which was boxing. That would make him fulfilled, he thought, so he formed the Mendoza Group.

Murray loved boxing, and he was good at it. The kid was a star of the University of Idaho boxing program. When he arrived at the 5th Street Gym, Hank Kaplan, the soft-spoken boxing historian, thought the name Gaby sounded too feminine. In a predominantly Jewish city, it would be better to call him Marty Kaplan. All of his fights thereafter were under that name. Murray had a great record, but he was a heavy puncher, and his hands were too delicate to take the pounding.

Luckily, Murray returned to his second love: art. Murray had top credentials there, having trained under an internationally famous painter named George Grosz.

Left to right: Ferdie, Murray Gaby, and Jimmy Ellis at the end of a fight. Luisita Sevilla Pacheco.

Still, the intense competition of boxing and the danger of the ring called to him. Nothing is quite like boxing. He missed the excitement of the boxing ring.

Murray put all of his many talents to work to devise a system to properly finance boxers, to give them adequate television and press exposure, and to match them (with the help of Chris Dundee) to a title shot. Murray's goal was to have at least one champion.

Murray got a group of reliable boxing veterans together to form a collection of teachers, corner men, trainers, and press men together in a group to be financed by Murray's friends, including John Baba, Gary Belcher, Charlie Crane, Steve Fisher, Joel Kruger, John Madden, Richard Marx, Albert Sokoisky, Dr. Leo Turmin, and Kurt Waldmann. This was the Mendoza Group. They were making good money and loved the excitement of big-time boxing in a glamorous setting in the Miami Beach Auditorium. Murray dug down deep in the history books and came up with the name Mendoza. Mendoza was the first Jewish champion during the bare-knuckle era and also, by the way, was the great-

great-great-great-grandfather of actor Peter Sellers. It was all handled with great taste, and Mendoza was a fitting title.

We headed to a party for the investors, and a few of the 5th Street Gym crowd came along. Nobody owned a tie or needed to.

Hank Kaplan, the gentle, genial boxing historian, gave an elegant, learned speech about Mendoza: who he was and what he meant to boxing. It was long and accurate.

Meanwhile, at the bar, Chris Dundee, the godfather of the Mendoza Group, was busily drinking himself into a fog. Free booze was something Chris could not turn down.

Hank was winding down his learned dissertation on who Mendoza was when Chris, glass in hand, wove to the front of the assemblage. Looking at the smashed Chris, Murray asked, "Chris, what is it?"

Chris grabbed the microphone and said, "What I want to know is who Mendoza was. I don't remember no Mendoza. Any group that starts out like that, you know is doomed to die. Who is Mendoza?"

The original group of boxing people included Dwaine Simpson, general trainer and conditioner; Chris Dundee, promoter; Hank Kaplan, who was the historian and critic for the 5th Street Gym; and the fight doctor with a connection at NBC boxing. A great team.

Murray's creative advertising sense took over. It was fun, and no one had ever seen such a show. We had cheerleaders, brass bands with uniforms, a glittering ringside audience, and a good boxing show. Initially our star was weak, though. We had a good local kid but no big matinee idol.

Marcel Clay, a middleweight, was brought in by Dwaine Simpson as co-manager and trainer of the fighters. Then Chris Dundee discovered Lou Esa and gave him to Michael Dundee, who brought him to Murray. Dwaine trained him also and was part of the contract. There is a full chapter on Lou Esa in my book *Blood in My Coffee*.

Then, through a gigantic stroke of luck, Murray landed a world-class middleweight. His name was Vince Curto, and the kid fit right into the Mendoza Group.

Vinnie Curto was a great boxer and a great entertainer. Boy, could he talk. He was a great con artist. He was better than anyone we'd had to

Don Johnson raising Vinnie Curto's hand in victory. *Left to right*: Roger Pinkeney, Chuck Talhami, Don Johnson, Vinnie Curto, and Frank Freeman. Jim Gestwicki.

date, and he was the next highly rated middleweight for the title. Curto was the goods!

He fought for us for over a year. His fights were great; he had a wonderful talent to box but not to fight. No toe-to-toe. He had the fluidity of motion that was hard to beat. He won every fight by a wide margin, with no knockouts—all unanimous decisions.

Murray took Angelo on board to help push Curto into a championship shot. Angelo would test him with top fighters in real fights. If Curto passed the stiff test, he would be ranked #1 for the title.

The first fight was in the Garden with Rodrigo Valdez, who was a Gil Clancy fighter. The first four rounds were a war. Then something clicked in Vinny's head in the fifth round, and he decided discretion was the better part of valor: he ran. Out-and-out running. He survived to an ugly loss, and he did not impress. "No heart," said the New York wiseguys. "No ticker." He was dismissed as a title prospect, and he still had three more tests to go!

In Philadelphia, Curto took on Bennie Brisco, a hard hitter. It was a battle, but Curto got severely cut and again quit. It was a draw; even that was a gift. He ended up with two huge cuts, which I sutured at Angelo's family's home. In the kitchen, the family women made pasta and sausages. Curto gathered further evidence that pain and suffering need not be part of boxing.

He fought and lost again, and finally we put him in with Tony Licata, who was Lou Viscusi's fighter. It was a hard-fought war and a losing effort, this fourth of the four test fights. He had also consolidated the thought that courage need not be a part of boxing. Never again would Curto take a hard fight. He retrained his con, his hustle. One backer after another fell for his jive, and years went by without a loss. He made his way west until he hit Hollywood and met Sylvester Stallone, who fell hook, line, and sinker for the likeable kid's spiel. Stallone tried to sell him to me at NBC.

"Here's what you are going to get. He'll work you for fifty thousand dollars and a Corvette sports car and a part in a movie, and then he will split," is what I told Stallone.

And that's the way it turned out. Vinnie wasn't a bad actor, but Sly wanted a good boxer. He had plenty of actors on his payroll, and it turned out I was right.

The Mendoza Group winner was a more reliable boxer: James Scott. Murray signed up Scott in Miami after he served time in Jersey.

As it always happens in boxing, a funny thing happened on the way to the title; they decided to parole James Scott to the custody of Murray Gaby in Florida. What a bad move that would prove to be!

James was ill prepared for freedom. He had been in prison since he was twelve years old, and he had no idea how to act. During the first days, no one could find him. Rumors ran wild that Scott had bolted.

Not so. When found, Scott was simply walking the streets, fascinated by his freedom. He was fascinated with Miami: the beach, the ocean, the bustle of Southwest 8th Street. He had not eaten in two days.

"Why not, Scott? You have money. You can eat at Wolfie's anytime—there you have an open tab. Why didn't you go?"

"Because nobody told me." Similarly, he had not gone to bed, because no one ordered him to.

Murray found himself up to his eyeballs with rehabilitation problems. As soon as Scott learned to use the phone, Murray inherited a round-the-clock phone partner. Scott called Murray for the most insignificant problems. Murray decided to move into a firehouse to ensure a night's rest.

Scott fought in Miami and did well. But he just couldn't adjust to being out of jail.

Murray made a mistake and bought Scott a car! He got him an old clunker, a Pontiac.

I tried to tell Murray that this was a piece of bad news. This guy is still under orders from his jailhouse bosses. Scott is out, Scott has a car, and Scott is eligible to kill anyone. Before you can say murder, Scott made a beeline for New Jersey, where his target awaited.

Scott shot his target right there on the street in front of a cop. He kept his gun on the seat with the spent cartridges on the floorboards and went on his way.

By the end of the day, he found himself in familiar surroundings: Rahway State Penitentiary. He was tried and convicted of murder.

Murray had a brother who was a powerful politician in New Jersey, and he got permission to let Scott fight while still in prison.

Since I was the boxing consultant at NBC, I could get NBC to cover the show in prison. Shocking! This had never been done before. So Gaby kept his career alive by promoting in prison.

For the first fight, we sort of snuck the kid on the air, expecting a monsoon of protest from a hostile press. We heard nothing. They were asleep at the wheel.

For that first fight, Scott asked me to work with him, as usual, and I did. NBC chose to replace me with heavyweight contender Ken Norton. Kenny was a massive man, very handsome, and was a big favorite with the kids. Later, Kenny said he felt like Marilyn Monroe walking into the penitentiary. He was a hunk of handsome masculinity, and the cons loved him.

From then on, I worked the NBC microphone and Scott did very well without me. The newspapers continued to ignore our experiment.

James Scott's corner and New Jersey corner men (unidentified). Luisita Sevilla Pacheco.

The problem was, we had nowhere to hide if they did question the propriety of having a career criminal fighting ranked fighters while doing time. There was no answer for that question. The warden, however, was all for the fights, since it helped his boxing program for cons. The gym was packed with aspiring cons hoping to get on NBC, some hoping to get out of jail. Boxing galvanized the prison. It was very healthy. Violence was down.

Scott took on the best opponent we could find who was willing to go into Rahway to face him. He faced mainly ranked contenders, and he beat them all. The boxing world sat up when he beat Eddie Mustafa Muhammad in an exciting ten-rounder. Who is this guy? Where's he going?

"To the championship!" we yelled, and the NBC brass were delirious with joy.

I had superb connections in Europe because my best friend in Europe, Jarvis Astaire, controlled boxing there at that time. English promoter Mickey Duff brought a good British boxer, Bunny Johnson, to fight Scott. Mickey gave the go-ahead to try to make a title match. Bunny Johnson had won fifty-two out of sixty-four pro fights. We were on the road to the title. Imagine a title fight in prison: first man to win the title while in jail! Bunny Johnson lost to Scott.

By this time, our NBC crews had been there so many times that they were on a first-name basis with the cons. A funny thing struck me when, once, we decided to take our wives to the prison. All of us were married to drop-dead good-looking wives. Mike Wiseman's wife, Carol, was a tall, leggy beauty with a sister equally as stunning. My wife, Luisita, was a flamenco dancer and stunning. Murray Gaby's wife, Julie, was a cover girl. Although apprehensive at first, they soon noticed that the cons were ignoring them and looking at our NBC crew of young, handsome men. This was the first time such a collection of beautiful woman had ever walked through a room packed wall-to-wall with young men and didn't hear a whistle or catcall.

Eventually, Scott ended his career when a former resident convict at Rahway, Dwight Braxton, fought Scott and retired him. The jail doors clanged shut on James Scott, a star attraction for the Mendoza Group and a contender for the light heavyweight championship of the world.

The fire burned out on Murray Gaby's amazing experiment.

The Mendoza Group had been a good idea, and we had our great nights. It was crazy and somehow a joy to look out at ringside and see a Who's Who of the Miami yuppies at ringside with the nice little cheerleaders and a brass band puffing away.

The Mendoza Group dismantled sadly. There would be no more exciting Tuesday nights, no more Embers Restaurant for a great meal, no more fights at the Miami Beach Auditorium and then, afterward, a victorious night snack at Wolfie's. The Mendoza Group was no more—and no more social events for the members.

The Mendoza Group died a peaceful death, which led to Chris Dundee standing in front of the auditorium, shaking his head. "I still don't get it. Who was Mendoza?" What a shame!

James Scott was released from prison in 2005.

14

The Cubans

At the very heart, the very core of the 5th Street Gym, in its peak years—the 1960s and 1970s—were the Cubans.

Chris had made a bundle off a flamboyant sizzling Cuban champion named Kid Gavilan, "The Keed," who boasted a flashing knockout punch called the Bolo Punch. It was a wind-up, sweeping uppercut. "The Keed" was available for Chris to use in a title fight, which the 5th Street Gym needed to bring life to the South Florida scene.

Chris's luck always seemed to work out because he had a kid who was the local darling. This one was a tall welterweight who was an expert boxer. He was also white. Bobby Dykes was his name.

The problem was that Miami was part of the segregated South. There was actually a rule prohibiting a bout between a white and a black man. Undaunted by the law, Chris signed the bout, and ticket sales took off. No one seemed to notice that a black man was going to fight a white man. Chris turned his hearing aid down and went about his business of hustling the super fight. "The Keed" came to town, and Hispanics packed the 5th Street Gym.

"It was ugly in those days," Chris said to me, remembering the night years later. "But I had some big boys behind me." Chris winked. And I read him loud and clear.

The Cubans *(left to right)*: Florentino Fernandez, Luis Manuel Rodriguez, Doug Vaillant, and Ultiminio Ramos. Enrique Encinosa Collection.

Blacks who came to see the fight could not stay in Miami Beach Hotels. The only way to see the fight was from the "Colored Section," which was called Parachute Seats.

Dykes, a very likeable young lad and clean as a whistle, was an emotional favorite. But the more realistic betting crowd had "The Keed" a 5–1 favorite, and betting was very heavy.

As Bobby Dykes's crew started to leave the dressing room, Bobby ducked into a toilet stall and had his left hand injected with Novocain by his dentist. Without the shot, Bobby would have had to fight a one-handed fight. Bobby went out and shocked the sellout crowd, who were treated to a wonderful, even-up title fight with a lead that seesawed back and forth.

At the end of the fight, the 5–1 bettors were counting their money. But somehow Kid Gavilan won wide—six points on two of the cards.

Castro Takes a Shot

In 1961, after another couple of years on the road, Luis Manuel Rodriguez got a rough fight: against Curtis Cokes in Houston. Luis Manuel trained diligently. He was ready. Curtis was tough, a good fighter, but he was not in Luis Manuel's class. Angelo and I looked at each other and said, "No problema."

I saw them off at the Miami Airport. Neither Angelo nor I would go until just before the fight.

The flight took off and promptly got hijacked to Havana. In their seats, Ernesto Corral and Luis Sarria were shocked. They knew they were on Castro's "Death List." They weren't sure about Luis Manuel. He would go to jail, perhaps, but it was not a death sentence.

Hours passed on the runway. Negotiations reached an agreement. They were cleared to take off.

Can you possibly imagine what that did to their preparation and concentration for a hard fight the next day?

Luis Manuel was a nervous wreck and could not sleep. Neither could Sarria or Corral. Angelo and I rushed in but were of no help. One minute you were facing death. Next night you were facing Curtis Cokes!

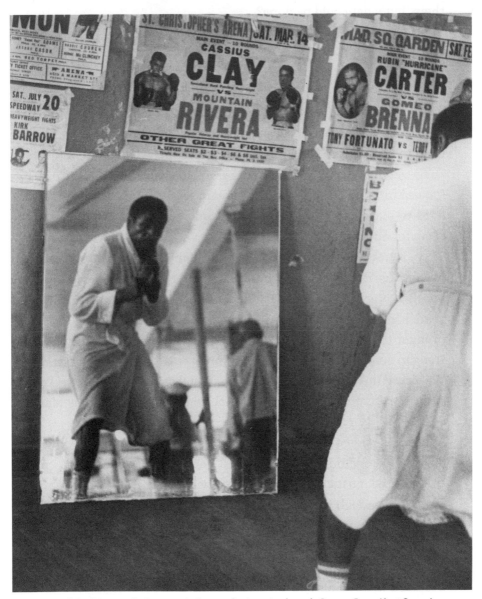

Luis Manuel Rodriguez shakes out in front of mirror in the 5th Street Gym. Kurt Severin.

Cokes won a decision, and it didn't even look hard. I felt so sorry for them, but what could be done?

Luis Manuel's luck was getting worse and worse.

No Roman Holiday

Years flew by with Luis Manuel winning steadily until he was signed to fight Nino Benvenuti, the great, if aging, Italian middleweight. Again we signed to go into the lion's den: Rome. Nino was king in Rome.

By 1969, Luis Manuel was getting worn and weary. He'd lost to Curtis Cokes in 19669–a fight lost in the steam room as Luis Manuel battled hard to make the welterweight limit and couldn't. Good luck didn't seem to want to come with us.

We snuck into Rome the back way and up to our hotel room on the freight elevator. To Luis Manuel, it was all the same, one country or another, one kind of spaghetti or another. It didn't matter. So many years had gone by. Luis Manuel was like an old Wild West gunslinger brought to town—as the opponent, to be slain by the favorite. Then the gun smoke cleared, and Luis Manuel was the only one standing. We picked up our check, tipped our hat, and said, "Adios, see ya' later." After the Castro call, *nothing* external would ever bother Luis Manuel again.

Rome is gorgeous. To fight in Rome amid the antiquities, with the Seven Hills of Rome spotlighted, all glitter, and witnessing a crowd that was the most elegant mixture of the movie and jet sets might not have been enough to impress Luis Manuel, but I was impressed.

Benvenuti was beginning to slide downhill, too, but the writers felt that Luis Manuel was farther along downhill: four title fights and over ninety career bouts. They questioned his strength and stamina and observed that he was getting old.

The fight went our way from the first round. For the first five rounds, Benvenuti lost every one. Luis Manuel's jab was a thing of wonder. Benvenuti didn't have the speed to hit Luis Manuel. Then Luis Manuel dropped down and brought up a smashing uppercut, and a huge gash opened on Benvenuti's forehead. "*Foul,*" cried the ref.

He came over and explained to an irate Angelo Dundee that to dip that way, to bend down at the waist, was considered in Italy to be a butt and was punishable by the loss of a point.

Meanwhile, across the ring, Nino's corner was administering first aid to the huge cut.

"Nobody is going to stop that cut," I said to Angelo. By then I had become the expert on cuts. Angelo, an expert himself, agreed. "But we're in Italy . . ." I nodded.

Luis Manuel had fought all ninety fights by bending at the waist and ripping uppercuts from that position. To take that away from Luis Manuel was to ask him to fight 50 percent different.

Also, if Luis Manuel was forced to fight standing up straight, he became vulnerable to hooks to the head, which happened to be Nino's best punch. It reduced Luis Manuel's defenses by 50 percent.

Meantime, Nino was a fountain of blood like the Red Sea, spraying the ringside crowd with a shower of blood. Repeated requests to have the ref go over and examine the cut with a ring physician resulted in brisk turndowns. In the States, the fight would have been stopped in the sixth round. We fought on. Luis Manuel was getting hit by hooks which never in his life had he been hit by.

Angelo made a decision—the only major mistake I ever saw him make in working with him for twenty years. It was a decision with which I in my heart fully agreed.

Luis Manuel was getting tired, too. It wasn't a sure thing that he could make it to fifteen rounds. Angelo looked hard into Luis Manuel's eyes.

"Luis Manuel, it's Rome, we can't win here. Nino is out on his feet. He's bleeding and weak. Can you give me one round at one hundred percent, all-out? Do you have it left to go hard?"

Luis Manuel nodded vigorously. He was a warrior. He knew not of quitting. He was used to finishing the show.

Nino felt the temperature change. There was no rest. Luis Manuel was on the all-out attack.

They met at the exact middle of the ring, under the lights. The crowd surged to their feet, feeling the end of the fight in sight.

Since Luis Manuel was fighting in a straight-up position and was vulnerable to hooks and since Nino decided to gamble it all on one powerful hook, the end was inevitable and the culmination of Luis Manuel's bad luck.

Luis Manuel was hit by Nino's last punch in his bag, a solid hook right to the point of the chin.

Luis Manuel folded like a beach deck chair, in sections, and remained seated but knocked out. It was the first time in more than ninety fights that Luis Manuel had gone down.

From there on out, and for years, Luis Manuel's fights continued in the same vein. He never tasted good luck.

If he had not experienced such a rash of bad-luck events, Luis Manuel could have been one of the greatest of welterweights—better than Kid Gavilan, better than Benny "Kid" Paret. Simply the best.

In the framework of this book on tales of the 5th Street Gym, I put Luis Manuel Rodriguez as the finest boxer of all who trained there, with the exception of Muhammad Ali. And after all, Ali was nothing but a blown-up version of Luis Manuel. They both fought the same; they were both superior boxers. Nobody came close to Ali. But he didn't have to deal with Luis Manuel's bad luck.

The Bad Luck of Luis Manuel Rodriguez

From the time Luis Manuel was young, his old, crippled uncle knew he was going to be the champion of the world. The problem was that the older man didn't know when.

The entire island of Cuba worshipped this quiet, unassuming, modest champ. He blitzed through the contenders and in no time was in line to fight for the championship. Then reality came and slapped him in the face.

The welterweight champ, named Don Jordan, was part American Indian. Jordan was owned by Frankie Carbo. The only way to get Luis Manuel to sign a contract was to give Frankie Carbo 50 percent of his contract if he won.

His uncle was deathly afraid of Norte Americano gangsters (and he was certainly right there). He would not sign the contract.

Frankie Carbo knew that the next guy to fight Jordan would beat him. Not only were his skills diminishing, but he was also an alcoholic. But Luis Manuel would not get the chance to knock Jordan out.

Carbo went to his second choice, Benny "Kid" Paret, whom Luis Manuel had beaten twice. A Cuban manager who was owned by Carbo owned him. No problema!

The match was made. Paret beat Jordan, and Luis Manuel was out in the cold. It would have taken a miracle to break into that Carbo circle.

The miracle came on New Year's Eve when Fidel Castro's *milicianos* swept into Havana and a new order was returned. Everyone hailed Castro as the new Abraham Lincoln.

Inside of one year, though, Castro showed his feathers, and they were pure red. Screams of "Paredon" (to the wall) meant death for those who did not agree with Fidel—thousands of Cuban dissidents. Batista was out! Gangsters were out! Meyer Lansky, Santo Trafficante were out! All the Cuban boxers left Cuba and went to Miami, where their new careers began.

In New York at the same time, an Island lad from the garment district was piling up victory after victory. His name was Emile Griffith, and a brilliant corner man named Gil Clancy trained him. Not only was Gil the smartest and best manager-trainer in New York, but he also had roots deep in Madison Square Garden and Teddy Brenner. What that meant was that Griffith would *never* lose a close decision in New York.

"Don't worry. I'll knock him out!" Florentino Fernandez never worried about decisions. His fights all ended by knockout. One way or another.

The fight was great. Emile was a wonderful fighter with a hard jaw. It was pretty even in the seventh round when Floro uncorked one of his devastating left hooks. Emile crumpled on the ropes. Not Gil, nor Teddy, nor any connection could help him. If he did get up, there was still thirty seconds to go, and Emile would not have been able to take what was coming to him from Floro. Never underestimate the power of New York. The ref picked up Emile by his gloves and proceeded to take the full thirty seconds to examine his gloves, talk to Emile, and make him walk around. The bell saved Emile.

SHOWERS

SUGAR BOY vs MARTY KAPLAN

IA   Ali

Floro

FLORO AND THE CHAM'
5TH ST GYM · LISTLO
pacheco 64   FIGHT

I looked at Angelo. He was green with rage. "If they can get away with *that,* imagine what they're going to do to us on the decision," I said in despair.

It came as no surprise: a Garden Griffith decision. The split decision was decided in Griffith's favor by one point. Floro lost.

Floro's popularity was so huge that Chris and Angelo were able to get him a middleweight title bout with Gene Fullmer, the tough Mormon warrior. The problem was that it would be in Utah in front of an audience of Mormons. The cards were stacked. Fullmer was a rough, tough tree trunk of a guy who was beating all the opposition, including a surprise win over the great Sugar Ray Robinson. But the betting fraternity saw Floro as too young, too strong, and too tough for the Battling Fullmer.

The only advantage Fullmer brought into the fight was that he was at home, in Utah, in Mormon country, with Mormon officials—which is like New York officials times two! Floro would have to KO the champ.

With the fight dead even in the thirteenth, Floro threw a devastating left hook and succeeded in breaking Fullmer's elbow. I can't imagine any more painful fracture. But what guts Fullmer had! He had to fight rounds fourteen and fifteen with a fractured elbow. We knew something was wrong, so we told Floro to go all-out on the elbow. Fullmer looked like he would faint from the pain. In the corner, he threw up. They wanted to stop it. Fullmer said no, that he'd gone this far. He would take three more minutes of inhuman pain. What a heart on Gene Fullmer! Floro was exhausted. He had gone all-out pounding the elbow. He had won the title, everywhere, except in Utah.

If it was even going into the thirteenth, then we took the last three rounds. They announced a split decision, with Fullmer keeping his title by a point. "That's a nice, fair Mormon decision," I said bitterly.

"Let's get outta here," Angelo said grimly. "If we stay any longer, the Mormons may hang us for good measure!"

Floro's KO power and his quiet, modest demeanor made him a TV fan favorite. Meanwhile, a tough gang fighter from the slums, a black fighter named Hurricane Carter, was building up an impressive skein of KO victories. The battle shaped up to be a war. As it turned out, it wasn't even a skirmish.

That night in the Garden I saw that Floro was distracted. His head was in Cuba. Rumors were floating around that night about an imminent invasion of Cuba by U.S. forces. Floro had to face Hurricane Carter. Hurricane didn't even know where Cuba was, much less that we were on the eve of World War III. His mind was on Floro.

I couldn't wake Floro up. He walked up the Garden ring stairs like a zombie. He had a vacant stare, as if he weren't really there.

"Uh-oh," I said to Dundee as the bell rang and we moved down the ring stairs. "He's asleep," I said. "His mind ain't here."

"It better be!" Angelo said, and BANG! Floro was down. Hurricane had landed a deadly left hook. Floro wasn't getting up.

"I hope the invasion has better luck," I said as we dragged him back to the dressing room. Poor Floro! It took fifty seconds!

Notwithstanding two first-round knockouts, Floro's popularity on TV soared. With the possibility of disaster in every fight, every fight was an exciting event. Floro fought on for many years, but he never reached that peak again despite fighting the most brutal series of fights ever seen on this planet at the end of his career.

The Garden and Gil Clancy bought in a monster-tough middleweight:

another Rocky, this one named Rocky Rivero. In his late twenties, he was not unbeaten when he fought Floro for the first time. His record was 48–8–1.

They fought four times, and each took two bouts. I never worked so hard sewing up fighters. Because of my friendship with Gil, I sewed up Rocky as well. Both of them seemed to enjoy the unbearable terror of the punishment. Rocky went home as a winner, but in time, he fell on hard times. And one night, depressed with how things were going, he committed suicide in Buenos Aires.

Floro looked sad when I told him the news. His take: "That's too bad. Now, I'll never be able to fight him again and see who would finally be best."

Of all the Cuban boxers, Floro took the biggest beatings, yet, today, Floro looks great. He appears ten years younger than his true age, doesn't talk or walk funny, and is still a happy-go-lucky kid and still a hero to the Cuban community.

The sad story of "Bad Luck" Luis Manuel stands in stark contrast. Without question, Luis Manuel was the best of the Cuban fighters. He was already the undisputed champion of all Cuba—amateur or pro. He had beat Benny "Kid" Paret and Kid Fichique for the Cuban welterweight title.

Meanwhile, the *next* best fighter in Cuba was Benny "Kid" Paret, whose manager was a restaurant worker who was definitely connected. Paret didn't have to be asked twice. He took Frankie's offer the first time it was offered.

Luis Manuel's uncle was on the list of Castro's enemies. So was Ernesto Corral, a bus-driver friend of the old man. Corrales was a corpulent, mild-mannered man who idolized and worked in Luis Manuel's corner. His name, it was rumored, was likewise on the "Death List."

The old man (who considered the bus driver with the snow-white skin as his son) called Corral to come as soon as he got the news of the Fidel Castro takeover. "You take Luis Manuel and Luis Sarria to Miami. You go see Chris Dundee. He'll get Angelo to work with you. These are honorable white men. With them, if you keep fighting like you are, they must give you a title shot. If Paret is the champion, Luis Manuel will beat him easy. Go—I give you Luis Manuel, and God bless you."

With no more than a handshake, a firm *abrazo* (hug), and a kiss, Ernesto Corral, bus driver on the #4 Route, stepped into the tall cotton and into a life of world travel and excitement.

But the bad luck of Luis Manuel kicked in. "Kid" Paret was a respectable champion. None could beat him. But in New York, where Gil Clancy was patiently grooming Emile Griffith, a match with the champion, Paret, was inevitable.

The first match was fierce. Griffith won a thirteenth-round knockout. The second was held on a night that was cold as hell with a heavy fog and sprinkles of rain. They filled up Shea Stadium. It was another fierce and very even fight. This time Paret won back his title. It was very close again, and the same wiseguys said that Carbo's hand was all over *that* decision.

No one could remember a fight with more hatred and vicious insults than the Paret-Griffith rematch. Paret had found out that Emile was a *maricon* (a homosexual), and he used that at every opportunity. Griffith, a good-natured kid, seethed and was going to defend himself. He admitted being gay and attended Gay Pride parades in New York.

The bad blood overflowed at the weigh-in. Paret was out of control. Anytime he came next to Griffith, he patted Griffith's bottom. Spotting Griffith's partner in the crowd, Paret pointed him out to the public and the press and said he would deliver Griffith back to him on a stretcher. And then, for good measure, Paret promised to kick the partner's ass.

The fight was fought at that low level—down and dirty. Here the first misstep was made by the New York State Athletic Commission. They appointed Ruby Goldstein, a premier referee but one just recovering from a major heart attack. He was too weak to physically control the infuriated fighters.

Time and again, the appointing of celebrity refs causes tragedy and mistakes. Once I saw Jerry Quarry take a huge beating from Joe Frazier which almost killed him. The ref was an old, weak champ, Joe Louis. He was pathetically lost. In my time, Ali won the second fight with Sonny Liston because the ref couldn't control a crazed Ali, who stood over Liston for seventeen seconds. The ref was Jersey Joe Walcott, a former heavyweight champion.

In the fateful round, Griffith caught Paret on the ropes. The attack was as vicious as I have seen. Paret slid along the rope as he was raked by heavy punches. Paret tried to pull himself up, but his arm hooked over the top rope, and he hung there splayed out like Jesus on the Cross. Where was Goldstein? He was late in coming and ineffective. Benny "Kid" Paret was pounded to death.

As an aside, let me make a medical observation. Old boxers usually die from the fight before the one that killed them. Benny Paret made a huge mistake in taking on Gene Fullmer, a thick, heavily muscled middleweight. Paret was a natural welterweight. Fullmer gave him a serious beating. A few months later, he took that swollen, beaten brain into the ring against Griffith. Who killed Paret: Griffith? Fullmer? Paret's manager? Or maybe Ruby Goldstein or all of them?

It took a long time for Griffith to recover from the guilt. Meanwhile, Luis Manuel waited. We weren't idle. Angelo had him on TV once a month. Luis Manuel was so good, he could fight bigger-weight fighters with complete confidence he could win. We fought a huge, mean Hurricane Carter and won twice. Bennie Brisco in their hometown of Philly. A tall Skeeter McClure in the Garden. All were big middleweights. Once Luis Manuel even fought and won easily against Vicente Rondon, who eventually became the Light Heavyweight Champion of the World! Still, we waited, fighting for short bread.

Finally, in 1963, the news came down. Luis Manuel would fight Griffith in Chavez Ravine. Also on the card was Ultiminio "Sugar" Ramos, who would fight Davey Moore, the "Springfield Rifle." Luis Manuel was a 3–1 underdog, and Ramos was 10–1. I took a nice roll of money to bet. I spent ten days in camp. It was my first time in a training camp. It was exciting. Hollywood stars dropped in. *Sports Illustrated* sent their top reporter, Mort Sharnik, to stay with us.

Bonding with the intelligent Sharnik, I studied what made journalism such an interesting profession. It was the first time that I had been bitten by the publicity bug. "Think of it," I would say every night, after I'd spent all day shepherding Mort Sharnik through Luis Manuel's workouts, eating with him at our training table, and spending time with the wound-up tiger, Sugar Ramos. "Think of it. My name in the *Sports Illustrated*."

I put down a huge bet that would pay my mortgage: $10,000 on Luis Manuel at 3–1; $5,000 on Ultiminio at 10–1. Wow!   Then we got up to face a monsoon of rain. Chavez Ravine was under three feet of water. The fight was a weekend fight. We postponed it until Thursday.

When the rain went down, so did the price. All of a sudden Luis Manuel went to even money: hardly worth a $10,000 risk. Ultiminio, my favorite bet, went from 10–1 to 5–1: worth a $1,000 bet but no more. I went from a possible $50,000 windfall to $6,000, which was hardly worth the sweat. I made a living betting on boxing. All during college, the service, and medical training, I made ends meet by betting. All of my big wins came when I was outside of boxing. After I was inside boxing, I quite betting on boxing, unless it was a bet I was sure was golden. For one reason or another, I never got *any* of the big bets down. My huge wins *would* have been Cassius Clay versus Sonny Liston, 8–1 for $10,000; Ali versus Foreman in Africa, 9–1 for $10,000; Luis Manuel versus Griffith #1, 5–1 for $10,000. It just wasn't meant to be.

We finished celebrating the win over Griffith, and we were not even out of the ring when Ultiminio "Sugar" Ramos came storming into the ring with fire coming out of his eyes. He looked like he was possessed.

Angelo was going to work the corner, and I followed him in like an unwanted anchor. Bear in mind, this was the first title fight I would work, and there were three that night. Three great fights in one night. I was thrilled!

Davey "the Springfield Rifle" Moore came into the ring cool and detached, as if he were out for a night's stroll. What he walked into was a mugging. For four rounds, it was a fierce give and take. In every round, Sugar seemed about to fall. At the end of the fourth, he came back so badly off balance that he was skipping on one leg like a drunken sailor on a storm tossed deck. I began to wonder when Angelo would stop the fight. But those were the days when no one stopped a fight. "You never know," they would say.

"Don't worry," said Sugar between puffy lips, blood pouring from his nose, both eyes closing, and his face full of lumps and bumps, "I got him now!" We looked at one another, and somehow we believed him! He was so sure of himself!

In the next round, things did change. Davey Moore slowed down. Now *he* was taking the beating. Savagely, Sugar mounted a two-fisted attack. Moore fell back, stumbled, and fell. In those days, there were only three ropes. A fourth rope (it's mandatory today) would have caught Davey's head. Instead he went back with full force and slammed into the floor with a sickening thud. Davey Moore lay still. The count went to ten, and Ultiminio "Sugar" Ramos was the new champion. Luis Manuel and I picked him up with Angelo. It was a moment of hysterical jubilation.

Unfortunately, it wasn't to last.

I went to see how Davey was in his dressing room. Mort Sharnik and his writer, Mark Kram, were in the silent dressing room.

Davey Moore sat up, put his hand to the side of his head, and said in a quiet voice, "My head really hurts." And he fell over.

To my experienced eye, Davey Moore was dead. Everyone rushed to the hospital, but of course, I was right.

Even this many years later I cannot express how I felt: first joy and exhilaration, then a devastating sorrow. And a devastating thought: What was I doing there? What kind of sport was I involved in? I, whose entire life was dedicated to saving life, to diminishing pain and suffering, was working a sport whose aim was to inflict pain and suffering whose unexpected end may be the death of the participant. For the next few months, I was very confused. I never did find an accommodation with the dichotomy of thought. I haven't to this day. I did get out of boxing when Ali wouldn't quit. I did network broadcasting, where I was allowed to campaign for boxing safety measures, such as the fourth rope, which might have saved poor Davey Moore.

But wait. Remember my theory about fighters who die because of the beating they took in the prior fight? Wait till you hear this one.

The story that came out of his camp many months later and was pretty much accepted by all of the people in his camp was this: Davey was a very popular champion. He spoke anywhere they asked him. However, his wife was a very jealous woman. She was always imagining that he was going to meet other women. It just wasn't so, for Davey Moore was a quiet man, not open to playing around.

One night he was invited to talk to a Boys Club. As usual, Davey was a huge success, and they kept him there for three more hours during questions and answers.

This put Davey back at his cabin after twelve o'clock. Waiting for him behind the door was his jealous wife, in a rage, holding a baseball bat. She struck him full force in the back of his head. He went over, completely knocked out. However, he did not go to the hospital, nor did he tell his manager. Only a few confidants knew, and because he appeared okay during training, they dismissed it.

If that story is true, then Davey Moore was a dead man going into the Sugar Ramos fight. He was a ticking time bomb.

So who killed Davey Moore? Was it Davey himself for not reporting the blow, or his wife for her savage attack? The confidants who didn't inform the manager? The doctor, for not making a more rigorous physical exam as he might have done had he known of the baseball bat blow?

Or, as Chris Dundee says, putting his palms up in a shrug, "What do you expect? It's *boxing!*"

I was more confused than ever. Boxing was wrong, but God help me, I love it so. And still, the bottom line was this: only boxers die.

In the aftermath, my tiny bubble of self-involvement burst. I'd spent weeks with Mort Sharnik collecting thousands of details for the Luis Manuel Rodriguez story.

Sports Illustrated went to their A-list to do a major cover story. It was the fight of the year, with plenty of backstory. Griffith's killing of Benny "Kid" Paret. Luis Manuel's narrow escape from Castro's "Death Lists." Carbo's involvement, which had made Luis Manuel wait four years for his chance. All great stuff.

In my naïve evaluation, the lovable Mort Sharnik was Mister Big New York journalist who was working so hard on the story. It was going to be BIG. I was going to be an important part of the story. For the first time in my life, I heard myself saying, "I . . . I . . . I . . ." and Mort Sharnik taking it all down in his notebook. Training in medicine, I had avoided any and all publicity. Imagine my ego blowing up. Boy, what would all my boyhood friends in Ybor City say? What would my doctor-pals say? I was fairly bursting with the joy of self-importance. The story became *not* Luis Manuel Rodriguez but, somehow, me! Me! Me! What a fool.

The day before the fight, a big awakening came in the form of the arrival of the *Sports Illustrated* first-string writer, Mark Kram. Kram looked exactly like Ernest Hemingway. Couldn't write like him, but he tried to. He was full of bluster and tough-guy demeanor and tried to do everything like Hemingway, except carry a shotgun.

Mort said cryptically, "He can write." Well, I sure hoped so.

Kram stayed up in the room frantically studying the thousands of pages of Mort's notes.

I grew to know Kram very well, and although he was hard to like, I grudgingly admitted that the man could write. As a Hemingway wannabe, he was dismal. As Mark Kram, boxing writer, he was the best. His stories of big events were masterpieces. In my funnel of real talent, I helped him whenever I could. And I learned from him.

So here was Kram, loaded for bear, with a super cover story of Luis Manuel Rodriguez, crammed full of colorful sidebar stories (courtesy of Mort) and waiting for a great fight, which Luis had to win, of course.

Luis Manuel did win. It was a sensational fight. It *would* have been a great story, but . . . The next fight was the story: "Ultiminio 'Sugar' Ramos kills Davey Moore."

Good-bye cover, good-bye Luis Manuel, good-bye Sharnik's thousands of pages of notes, good-bye Angelo, good-bye Dr. Pacheco. My brief moment in the sun of national publicity was over before it began.

Kram pushed Sharnik aside and pulled me into the cab to head to the hospital.

Kram traveled a lot with us during the Ali days and with Jimmy Ellis. During a location frolic, I fixed him up with a Filipino beauty who had been turned down for the Ali harem because she was too light skinned.

Kram, for all his trying to act like Hemingway with the ladies, was a figure of ridicule to them—a horrible bust. Once I fixed him up with a gorgeous Swedish hooker in Stockholm. She cost a hundred dollars, but nevertheless he fell in love and wanted to take her to New York. "Not even if you *were* Hemingway," said Sara the Swede, and Kram went back to soothe his bruised feelings with his wife, his three kids, and his Jewish mistress.

The Philippine girl, though, wanted to come to America to stay, to study, to succeed. She was very pretty and extremely sexually aggressive. Kram fell so hard that he took her to New York City, falling out with the wife and the kids and the mistress. This suddenly presented him with a cash-flow problem.

Enter Don King and Paddy Flood. They bought Kram, and they thought *Sports Illustrated* went with the sale.

An investigation by Mort Sharnik revealed an extraordinary tale. Out went Mark Kram. Good-bye to the Filipino (who is still here, running for Congress, I hear), to Don King and Paddy Flood, to wife, kids, and mistress, to the Hemingway disguise, to the big time—hello to obscurity and poverty.

He died recently, broke. Before he did, though, after all the years of talking about it, he wrote a book on, I believe, Ali in Manila. He would know . . .

The New York Blues

We returned to Miami after winning the title in L.A., and Luis Manuel was swept into a different world, that of celebrity-hood. Everyone wanted a piece of this quiet, humble kid. There were parties every night.

Up to that point, Luis Manuel had lived a sensible, orderly existence. He had found a beautiful Cuban girl, Lourdes, who was graduating as a Licensed Practical Assistant, which in Cuban hospitals was the equivalent of a Registered Nurse. Through thick or thin, the beautiful, shy, quiet girl would stick resolutely to Luis Manuel. He would come over and ask me about life in the United States. I told him, above all, to buy a house and pay for it. The house should be modest, new, and in a neighborhood he was comfortable in. He should pay for it out of his boxing money. I believe that he found the right house, paid $20,000 for it (the price of a good middle-income house at that time), and lived in it until he died. That much he did right.

Everything was coming up roses, and then the old gang stuck it to Luis Manuel. Most boxers who win the title get a reprieve of six months or so to have a couple of easy fights to bag $50,000 or more, to "put money in the bank."

Before Luis Manuel could contemplate the first easy fight, though, Chris called Angelo and said, "Get him ready. He's fighting Emile Griffith in the Garden in a month!"

What? We all looked at each other. Here was our six-month rest to make money. Luis Manuel had, for the first time in his life, allowed himself to get wildly out of shape. This was suicide. Emile was unbeatable in the Garden: we had seen that with all of our fighters.

I couldn't get a straight answer from Chris. How could I? Let's look at the cast of characters. You have the Clancy, Griffith, and Teddy Brenner connection interfacing with Chris, Carbo, and a TV network that needed a big attraction. Bingo! It was a done deal.

It was a shameful sellout.

Even Angelo had to resort to a rationalization to justify the fight. "It won't make any difference. This time we knock him out!" It sounded lame to me.

With heavy hearts, we went to New York to get jobbed again. This time, though, Luis Manuel's bad luck kicked in. The sycophantic fans had bombarded the impressionable Luis Manuel that this time he didn't need his left jab and boxing. This time he would knock Emile out with a right hand. Luis Manuel believed it completely.

Luis Manuel, who always before had listened carefully to the corner advice from Sarria and Angelo, turned a deaf ear. For the first five rounds, Luis Manuel did not throw a jab, his best weapon. He hunted an elusive Griffith, looking to land a hard right hand. The problem was that he didn't have a hard right hand. Luis Manuel knocked people out by landing a blizzard of punches in bunches. No one could resist his flashing combination. He didn't have one-punch knockout power. He was no Florentino Fernandez.

By round six, we were down 5–0 and in New York! When we finally woke Luis Manuel up, it was too late, although the next ten rounds were almost all for Luis Manuel. Luis Manuel won the fight 8–7 on all press cards, but they don't count. New York judges saw it for Emile. Luis Manuel had held the crown for three months. He came out of two fights with a new house (paid for) and a new Pontiac convertible worth $2,000 in those days.

The fair-weather crowds melted away, and life returned to normal. Gil Clancy was in no hurry to return the favor, and Luis Manuel hit the road again. Griffith had his easy fights.

Emile Griffith versus Luis Manuel Rodriguez in Las Vegas

Eventually he had to fight Luis Manuel again, though. This time he got a fair shake; he went to fight in Las Vegas at the big auditorium.

All went well except that a Santeria priest layered on, as Cubans are very superstitious. Sarria, Corral, and Luis Manuel bit hard.

The next chapter of Luis Manuel's hard luck quickly kicked in. We were in a gridlock line of cars going to the auditorium on a steaming afternoon.

Suddenly Luis Manuel said in a voice of panic, "We forgot the blessed coconut. We got to go back!"

After a brief moment of panic, an assistant said, "I packed it in the trunk."

All doors opened, and we opened the trunk, equipment flying and cops converging on the limo. Horns were blasting and tempers were short.

Then came the big problem: how to split a coconut. We tried tire irons, dropping it on the road, everything. More time passed; more horns blew; more cops descended. But Luis Manuel wouldn't budge unless we opened the coconut and he drank the milk from it. No Luis Manuel, no fight. Thousands waited at the auditorium, and millions more at home were watching TV.

What to do?

A burly Nevada state trooper pulled out a huge magnum pistol. It looked like an artillery piece. Everyone jumped on him. "God, no! You want to cast a spell? You want negative mojo?"

Finally, someone found a giant screwdriver. Pounding it with the butt of the magnum, we cracked the coconut and Luis Manuel drank his coconut milk. He was not totally happy, but there it was, a bad beginning of a hard fight.

The Santeria priest was right. The episode produced a bad mojo. For the first time in three fights, Luis Manuel really lost the fight with Griffith, 8–7 again, with Teddy Brenner nowhere in sight. Luis Manuel just flat lost. Unfortunately, his bad luck was just beginning.

My Education

Ramiro Ortiz

Ramiro Ortiz represents a generation of immigrants who came to this country and grew up here. His generation exploded to make a South Florida renaissance a reality. They turned their hands to the young Cuban immigrants and stamped their progress.

Ramiro came from a strong, secure Cuban family who believed strongly in family, country, patriotism, and hard work. They all prospered and they all succeeded. But that was not enough. Their children had to follow in their footsteps, and they, too, had to succeed.

Ramiro grew up with everything in his favor. He had very strong good looks, athletic skills, and a good brain. He was destined for success.

But an insidious drop of boxing landed in his blood. Ramiro wanted to box. He had a great physique, great courage, ambition, and the willingness to pay the price. His father was horrified. A boxing future was not what his father had in mind.

Fortunately, Ramiro's talents were not commensurate with his lofty ambitions in the ring. He was good—not great—and he was smart enough to know that.

His intelligence served him well on the banking side of his life. Ramiro as a young man was already marked as a "comer." He was recruited, and his advancement ran ahead of even the most optimistic expectations. Ramiro Ortiz was going to be somebody in banking.

One more brush with the dying fire of boxing expectation occurred, though, and Ramiro decided to link up with Hank Kaplan, the aged ring historian, to promote fights in Fort Lauderdale after Chris Dundee had folded. They struggled mightily, but neither man was a Chris Dundee. A boxing promoter is a rare find. Neither Hank nor Ramiro had the genes. First of all, they were too nice, and second, they were too honest.

Their journey came to a halt when I wanted to help Ramiro and gave him a televised fight on NBC. It was a small summer fight, and I wanted to put his name before the national boxing nation.

One Sunday morning I got a panic call from NBC. Our main-event fighter had run away to California. We had a 3 p.m. TV date and no main event!

I came to find out that the fighter had a fight with his trainer. In a huff, the fighter hopped a bus for California.

I patched up a fight but had a long talk with Ramiro. "Son, a banker you are and a fight promoter you ain't."

Ramiro returned to banking; today he is one of the most successful bankers in Miami. Ortiz is the president of Bank United.

Not able to stay away entirely from boxing, he is also a top executive on the Florida Boxing Commission.

My father wanted me to be an accountant. When I was a child, he would spend his time reviewing addition, subtraction, and multiplication with me. My grandfather would tell me about Jack Dempsey, Battling Nelson, Henry Armstrong, and the great Kid Chocolate. Needless to say, my grandfather got my attention.

My earliest recollection of boxing was a picture my grandfather showed me of Jack Dempsey. It immediately captured my imagination: his fighting pose, his look, his build. This man was a hero! A hero for doing what I got into trouble for—fighting. Wow! I was hooked.

Our life was good in those days. A big house in the Miramar suburb of Havana, Cuba, and weekends at either the Miramar Yacht Club or at my grandfather's ranch (and to boot—his boxing stories)!

Little did we know that our world was about to turn completely upside down. With Fidel Castro in power, we soon would be leaving Cuba for exile in the United States.

Upon our arrival in the United States in 1960, we lived in Hialeah for two years. Three families lived in one small house. What days those were! About a year after our arrival, a magic box came to our house: a television set! Everybody in our house had a different program they wanted to watch, but my grandfather and I shared an interest in the

Ferdie and a young Ramiro Ortiz. Ferdie Pacheco Collection.

"Friday Night Fight of the Week." My education was about to start! Let's call it elementary school.

Every Friday night was magic. Gene Fullmer, Dick Tiger, Carmen Basilio, Sugar Ray Robinson, and the special treat—Luis Manuel Rodriguez, Florentino Fernandez, and Benny "Kid" Paret. When Luis Manuel or Florentino or Paret fought, the world would stand still. Everybody came to watch. Many fights were memorable. I still maintain that my first English teacher was the great boxing commentator Don Dunphy.

The one match that made the most impression was obviously Emile Griffith versus Benny "Kid" Paret. In the twelfth round, when Benny slid down the ropes during a savage beating, I remember my grandfather saying, "This man will never get up again." Unfortunately, he was right. Many years later, when I reflected back on that moment, one thing came to mind on how I felt at such a young age watching that horrible tragedy. I remember thinking, "This is boxing. This is the risk you take." Incredibly, each and every time they climbed into the ring elevated my respect for these athletes. To this day, it bothers me tremendously when a fighter is ridiculed in the ring. There was also a sense of revenge: of expecting that Luis Manuel Rodriguez would get even for Benny "Kid" Paret. (In 1963 he did!)

At the end of 1962, we moved to Miami Beach. Unbeknownst to me at the time, my education would presently go into high gear. Let's call it high school.

We moved into a run-down apartment building on 39th Street. The entire building was made up of Cuban exiles like ourselves. My first priority was to find out who had a television set and whether any of them were boxing fans. If so, I needed a way to find and meet them. Happily, I learned quickly that Friday night fights were religion in this building. In one of the apartments, the men gathered around the set, and I was quickly accepted into the group.

Next to the apartment building was a parking lot with a small shed for the attendant. On the wall, I saw magic: boxing posters! Right before my eyes were the pictures of the very heroes I saw on TV: Willie Pastrano, Ralph Dupas, Sugar Ray Robinson, a young Olympic champion named Cassius Clay, and of course my favorites, Luis Manuel Rodriguez and Florentino Fernandez. It was in these posters that a picture got my attention—Chris Dundee. This was the man who put it all together! This was the promoter!

I was immediately challenged. How do I go to the Miami Beach Auditorium to see a boxing show? If a ticket cost a dollar, I couldn't have smelled one. After several Tuesday fight nights "scouting the auditorium," we figured it out. We would do our best to blend in with the fighters as they entered the auditorium. We would pick up a fighter's bag or robe or anything to blend in. Once inside, it was easy; just stay away from Chris Dundee, who we were sure would boot us out. One particular night I'll never forget—we were in Luis Manuel Rodriguez's dressing room and Angelo Dundee had allowed us in! To our terror, five minutes later Chris walked in. "Did they buy tickets?" (First things first for Chris.) "Who the hell are these kids?" We panicked. Angelo defiantly told Chris, "These are reporters from Peru," and winked at us. Some reporters—we were thirteen years old! (If I live to be a hundred, I'll never forget that moment. Thanks, Angie.) Chris looked at us and was off to find other "dead-heads" (a term used by Chris Dundee to describe somebody who had not paid for a ticket).

All along, my education was vastly improving. My literature lessons had become clear: *Boxing Illustrated* and *Ring* magazine. What an education for a thirteen-year-old Cuban refugee.

Now that my education was advancing, I had a new challenge: how do I get to visit the 5th Street Gym, the mecca of boxing?

On a Saturday morning, we set out on an adventure. A bus went to Washington Avenue and 5th Street, and transportation was resolved! When we got there the entrance looked like a cave. You just saw darkness. Soon, we realized the darkness was a rickety wooden stairwell that creaked with every step. I was careful and deliberate, soaking all this in, when a blur ran by me, up the stairs. My heart stopped. It was Douglas Vaillant, the #1 lightweight contender! We were there! Our next challenge came immediately. A short man right out of central casting with a stubby, chewed-up cigar clenched between his teeth mumbled, "Two bits." I had prepared myself for almost everything but that. First, what in hell is "two bits"? Second, once he translated and told us it was a quarter to get in, we had a major decision to make. We each had a quarter, but that was bus fare for the ride home. What to do? The decision was easy: my two buddies turned around and walked out. I did a rapid risk assessment. I was already there. I was immediately hypnotized with the rat-tat-tat sound of the speed bags, the thumps of the heavy bags, that pat-pat-pat of the jump ropes on the wooden floors, and most of all, the sound of leather hitting flesh in the ring. I looked around, and before my very eyes stood Willie Pastrano with Angelo Dundee arranging his headgear. Luis Sarria was working on Luis Manuel Rodriguez. Nothing would get me to leave! I would walk home (thirty-five blocks). Good decision. I was now taking advanced courses.

In the weeks to come, Saturday mornings hanging out at the 5th Street Gym became a special treat. It was there that my two main textbooks, *Ring* magazine and *Boxing Illustrated,* came to life. Imagine reading the *Count of Monte Cristo* and having Edmond Dantès appear in your living room!

Amidst this wonderful world of the Miami Beach Auditorium and the 5th Street Gym, there was one fellow who didn't fit in; yet he was so different that he did indeed fit in! I was to learn that he was Dr. Ferdie

Pacheco—a Hispanic just like me! I marveled at the ease with which he would blend in with the toughest of those characters—Lou Gross (one of the most famous occupants of the gym), Chris and Angelo Dundee, the fighters themselves—and with the many celebrities who would come to the gym on a regular basis. Rich or poor, famous or infamous, black or white didn't matter to him. He was the same with all. I wanted someday to be like him, a respected member of the community yet one who was at home with royalty or beggars (you saw both at the 5th Street Gym).

Once again, my world was about to turn. My family informed me in late 1964 that we were moving to Fort Lauderdale. Fort Lauderdale? There isn't any boxing there, I thought. There aren't any boxing gyms. Why would we move to Fort Lauderdale? As we prepared for the move, I made the best phone call I ever made in my life. Among the 5th Street Gym regulars, the nicest, most approachable guy was Hank Kaplan. His role at the gym was simple, although he managed a couple of fighters: he was the expert. If you needed information you went to Hank. Even Chris Dundee went to Hank. I told him on the phone who I was, and we talked boxing for thirty minutes. I fell in love with this guy. Here was one of Chris's guys who actually took a fourteen-year-old boxing fanatic seriously.

After we moved to Fort Lauderdale, certain priorities became essential. First, where was there a newsstand where I could buy *Ring* magazine and *Boxing Illustrated*? Next was finding somebody with a car that could actually make it to Miami Beach and turn him into a boxing fan. Over time, all three were accomplished. I had learned a thing or two about goal setting.

At age sixteen, I experienced two important events. First, I got my license and an old Oldsmobile, with enough jugs of water in the trunk that would take care of an engine that constantly overheated but would usually make it to Miami Beach. Second, we set up a boxing ring in my backyard. Four stakes dug into the ground, three strands of rope, and presto! I had a ring. An old straw-filled footrest secured by wooden crates, and I had a heavy bag. An old piece of rope, and I had a jump rope. I was in business! My education was rising to the next level.

I soon had regular bouts scheduled in my backyard. It was the most convenient arena you ever saw. It was in back of a shopping center, and the crowd would circle around my backyard. Boxing had arrived in Fort Lauderdale.

Word of our backyard bouts soon spread. We received an invitation from a fellow in Hollywood who went by the name of Kid Pantonio. In a West Hollywood church complex, he was conducting CYO Boxing shows. If we drove our Fort Lauderdale team there twice a month, he would put on a boxing show. In addition, he would give us some pointers, which we readily accepted. The matches were even for the most part, and most important, we were boxing in a real ring (almost). One thing didn't make sense, though. He was supposed to be helping us, yet he was working the corners for the Hollywood boys. Something wasn't kosher. After a couple of months, the church got out of the boxing business.

My early boxing career soon turned into a no-win situation. If I won, my mother was upset, for she was sure that my opponent with a bloody nose or mouth would sue us. If I lost and I was the one bruised up, my father would look at me with disdain and ask, "What kind of accountant are you going to make?"

Eventually life took me to Broward Community College, a computer programming education, and the start of my banking career, but once again I had difficult decisions to make. Tuesday night fights in Miami Beach were still a priority, but I was operating computers on the evening shift. What to do? For the first time in my life, I put boxing aside. I would focus on my banking career. Soon I was on the day shift and right back to the Miami Beach Auditorium on Tuesday nights.

It was the early 1970s. There was a new hero in town. Luis Manuel Rodriguez and Florentino Fernandez were fading. Age and too many wars were catching up with them, but Frankie Otero, from Hialeah, was the new idol. One of us! The young Olympic champion Cassius Clay was a bona-fide legend called Muhammad Ali. I was getting my college education. I had even started a new math program—the Ring Record Book. I would go to the fights but was as interested in watching and observing Chris Dundee as I was the fighters. I once again started to blend in, though not as a starry-eyed thirteen-year-old but as a young man in his twenties interested in learning the business side of boxing.

On fight night, I watched Chris Dundee work the crowd. He was on top of everything: who was sitting where, who was sitting next to whom, who was in attendance, and the reaction of the crowd to different fighters. I was soaking it in. Progressing through my college education in boxing, I became very close to Hank Kaplan (who had suggested I focus on an education and forget boxing). I visited him whenever possible, and he was warm, receptive, and always willing to go to the gym on a Saturday morning and talk boxing for as long as I wanted. He formally introduced me to Dr. Ferdie Pacheco. I would ask Ferdie questions incessantly about Ali, his travels, Luis Manuel Rodriguez, and Florentino Fernandez. Ferdie (big-shot Ferdie) was only too happy to talk boxing. What days!—and the 5th Street Gym, always the 5th Street Gym. I would go there on Saturday mornings with Hank. What magic! There was Muhammad Ali himself, training, joking, sweating, dancing; Roberto Duran beating up a poor hapless sparring partner; Vito Antuofermo; Wilfred Benitez; Wilfredo Gomez; and a new up-and-coming welterweight who had won a gold medal in the Montreal Olympics, Sugar Ray Leonard.

I had by then developed a relationship with all the gym regulars, from Sully, Larry Golub, and Mac Goodman to Moe Fleischer (better known as "Sell-Out Moe" to the fight crowd; I lovingly called him my "Jewish grandfather"!) to Hank Kaplan and Ferdie Pacheco to the fighters themselves. I was getting a sense of the business by managing a couple of preliminary fighters that not even Sully or Mac Goodman would mess with, unless I handed them twenty dollars to bandage the fighters' hands and work the corner. It was almost perfect, but one thing was lacking; I needed to figure out a way to develop a relationship with the dean of this campus of higher learning—Chris Dundee. The answer was obvious. I offered to sell tickets to his Miami Beach shows, in Fort Lauderdale! "What do you want from me in return?" he asked in a raspy voice. "Nothing," I said. "Just give us good seats." He smiled at me and hugged me, and we were friends for life.

Ramiro Ortiz *(left)*
and Moe Fleischer.
Jim Gestwicki.

In 1981, I took the next step in my boxing education: I would go to
graduate school and earn my MBA in the Sweet Science. I convinced
Hank Kaplan that he and I should promote professional boxing shows
at the War Memorial Auditorium—the student and the professor together, I told him. Hank agreed. After months of negotiating with the
City of Fort Lauderdale for the use of the War Memorial Auditorium,
we had a deal. We were on our way. Boxing in Fort Lauderdale had
graduated from the back of the Riverland Shopping Center to monthly
shows at the War Memorial Auditorium.

We were putting our first show together. There I was sitting across from Angelo Dundee, negotiating to use one of his fighters, Greg Sorentino, in our main event. Pinch me, is this really me?

Saturday mornings at the 5th Street Gym took on a new meaning. The same people I used to pester and ask questions of would now come to me. We would argue as we negotiated over a four-round fight, and I would try hard not to smile. I didn't want to blow my cover (Chris Dundee would have never smiled, negotiating a six-rounder with Lou Gross!). After our second show, Chris Dundee called. He wanted to have dinner. He wanted to be my partner! I was trying my level best to negotiate a good deal for Hank Kaplan, and I couldn't let Chris know that I would have paid him to join us. Eventually a deal was done. It was now the student, the teacher, and the dean of the school promoting monthly boxing shows at the War Memorial Auditorium. Chris's first lesson: "Never, never give away a ticket. Don't ever create a dead-head." I tried hard not to smile. I never did tell him about the reporters from Peru.

Those three and a half years promoting boxing may have been the most enjoyable years of my life. Every Wednesday night Chris Dundee and I had dinner. Hank joined us when he could. I learned more about life at those Wednesday dinners with Chris than I could have learned at Harvard University. Those Wednesday nights will always be cherished. Chris's insights on life, on problems, on opportunities, on people, and on business were invaluable. Twenty years later, I still think about lessons from Chris while dealing with day-to-day problems.

We promoted over thirty shows: some good ones, some stinkers, some championship shows (including the junior featherweight fight in Miami Beach between Sergio Palma and Leo Cruz), and some failures, such as on an *NBC Sports World* show with Dr. Ferdie Pacheco, when one of our main-event fighters left town (unbeknown to any of us). Through it all, I was in boxing, a full-fledged member of the fraternity.

My banking career continued to grow, and in 1984 my life came to a crossroads. My employer, SunTrust Bank, had acquired Flagship Bank. It was the largest bank merger in the country at the time. I was asked to head up the project, and it was too important an opportunity to

Ramiro Ortiz (*left*) and Roberto Duran at the 5th St Gym. Ramiro Ortiz collection.

pass up. I quickly accepted the challenge, knowing that my days as banker by day, boxing promoter by night had come to an end. My days of two full-time, demanding jobs were over. During the next couple of years, I managed a few fighters on the side (the most notable ones were Johnny Goodwin and Jose Guzman), but the challenges of my bank job were just too demanding for me to do justice to the fighters that I was managing, and I gave it up.

The good news? My banking career flourished. The bad news? I would miss "fight nights" more than anyone would ever know. Unfortunately, in the late 1980s, Chris Dundee had a stroke and died several years later. At his funeral, many of the crowd from the glory years of the Miami Beach Auditorium and the 5th Street Gym were there. All the assorted characters. A newspaperman covering the funeral asked me, "What did Chris mean to all of you?" I simply looked at him and said, "Chris was the glue that held this wonderful world together."

It is now 2007. Many of the people in this story are gone. Luis Manuel Rodriguez has passed on, and so have Willie Pastrano, Moe Fleischer, Luis Sarria, Lou Gross, Larry Golub, Sully, and the incomparable announcer Frank Freeman. Characters like Buddy Gilbert, Marty Goldstein, Ben Lonic, George "Tiger" Small, and Hank Kaplan are also gone, but the friends I made in boxing, members of the Sweet Science fraternity, I love and cherish their friendship still today: friends like Enrique Encinosa, Ferdie Pacheco, Angelo Dundee, Frankie Otero, Murray Gaby, Tommy Torino, Roger Pinckney, and so many others.

Dad, I'm sorry I didn't make it as an accountant. Instead, I became president of Bank United, the largest bank headquartered in the state of Florida. But did I ever tell you about the time Roberto Duran (135 pounds) knocked down Vinnie Curto (160 pounds) at the 5th Street Gym using fourteen-ounce gloves?

Old Hands in the Gym

Tom Archdeacon

Well-travelled sports columnist for the *Miami News* during the heyday of Ali, Tom Archdeacon now is in Dayton, Ohio, churning out his unique columns on sports. This article was excerpted from a 1977 column in the *Miami News.*

The cold spell that crept into Miami the other day found it easy to take over the 5th Street Gym. The place has no heat, and for most of the day it stands empty.

When the regulars finally tromped up the stairs and into the gym just before lunch on Monday, they wore cardigan sweaters, wool shirts buttoned up to the neck, and caps to cover their balding heads.

None of the fighters had begun their workout, so the men plopped down in the old red theater seats that line the south wall of the gym. That's where the rays of noonday sun poured through the grimy windows and danced on their backs until their bodies were soon as warm as their memories.

The men sat in a row like old birds lined up on a telephone wire. Moe Fleischer, the fellow they called "Sell-Out Moe" in New York a half a century earlier, wore a sport coat and carried his soggy-tipped cigar between his fingers.

Next to him sat veteran trainer Mac Goodman, a watch cap pulled over his ears, with his hands as in prayer, folded in front of his face.

A young Tom Archdeacon with Ferdie. Luisita Sevilla Pacheco.

They hid parts of his salt-and-pepper mustache and the tinted glasses he wore for his sensitive eye. Years ago, when the place was an Italian restaurant, not a gym, he said he brought his mother here to eat.

Jerry White, the grand storyteller of the bunch, wore his clip-on sunglasses flipped skyward so that they nearly touched the old white cap that has become his trademark. He was shoulder to shoulder with Allie Ridgeway, his friend of fifty-six years.

Ridgeway, a great lightweight fighter during the depression, wore a brilliant yellow sweater and a sporty straw hat that covered his white hair. Only his nose, given a few roller-coaster curves thanks to his day in the ring, gave hint that he had once been a two-fisted pug.

At the end of the row sat Larry Golub. With his black horn-rim glasses, the wisps of hair that swirl across his head, and his serious look, he could pass for a professor. It is only when he works the corner of a boxing ring that he takes on the airs of a doctor. He carries a black physician's bag, and when a battered boxer suddenly stumbles onto his stool, Golub's old hands work with surgical precision.

The bunch hadn't been sitting five minutes when the kibitzing began. "What do you mean, Moe?" Ridgeway asked incredulously. "I'm seventy-four. How can I be seventy-eight? When I was fighting you used to call me mister. You don't call a man your same age mister! I'm the youngest guy here!"

Goodman shook his head in disagreement but did not speak.

"I'm the oldest one here," said Fleischer. "Only Sully has a year on me. But you're close to Allie."

White put the needle into his buddy a little further. "That's right, Moe. Remember how Allie was our idol."

It wasn't long until a couple of fighters began loosening up in the ring. That's when the young black guy with the flashy three-piece suit made his entrance. He wore a white silk shirt with French cuffs and a black fedora with the brim turned down. He had on sunglasses, and he had both a toothpick and a cigar wedged between his teeth. A scar crept down the side of his face.

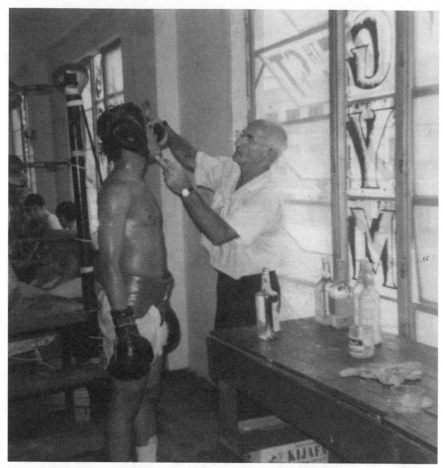
Larry Golub putting headgear on the Louisville Kid. Jim Gestwicki.

He did not speak but headed straight to the side of the ring, where he began peering intently at the fighters. He held a newspaper in his hands behind him. Soon he was rocking to the motion of one of the fighters, dodging imaginary punches and grimacing with each exaggerated move.

The old men watched and began to chuckle.

"Sometimes the guy comes in screaming and raving, other times he shadowboxes in silence," said Billy Sheridan, the tattooed ex-fighter who ran the gym for Chris Dundee. "Sometimes he comes up here with a bicycle, other times he's wearing just a swimming suit." Sheridan chuckled to himself. "By looking at this get-up I guess he musta had some stocks come in."

White nodded toward the fellow. "He's a throw-back to the twenties. That's how some of those guys used to look in Stillman's Gym in New York. There's always something about a gym- -it draws characters like honey draws flies."

They all agreed, but in truth the looking glass should be held on them, not the guy in the three-piece suit. He is nothing more than an eccentric misfit. These men, along with fellows like Lou Gross and Emmitt Sully and Chuck Talhami, are the characters of the place.

They are as much a part of the 5th Street Gym as the heavy bags and the rundown tables and the boxing ring. They give the place its color and soul. They are the link between boxing's golden era and today.

They have years of experience. Sully is eighty-one, Fleischer eighty. The rest are in their seventies, except for the three youngsters—Goodman is sixty-seven, Sheridan fifty-five, and Talhami, the baby of the bunch, is thirty-eight.

Pinball kings *(left to right)*: Emmitt Sully, Larry Golub, and Moe Fleischer. Jim Gestwicki.

They have had a hand in the development of nearly every boxer who has ever come through the doors of the 5th Street Gym, from the greats like Muhammad Ali and Carmen Basilio and Sonny Liston to the kids who now work out there daily. They have trained fighters, managed them, and worked as seconds and cutmen. They have endless tales, they exaggerate gossip and bicker with one another, and yet they come together at noon early every day of the week, year after year. The place is more than a gym to them—it is a social club.

"Boxing is a responsibility, but it can also be fun, and I've had a lot of it with this business," said Ridgeway. "It makes me feel good when I walk in here. This place brings back memories. There is so much you get out of walking into a place like this, and it all comes from fellows like we have here."

No one is as colorful as Billy Sheridan—literally. His arms are covered with tattoos. When he was in the service, he had the naval emblem engraved on his left bicep, the eagle on his right. A bare-chested hula girl dances down one forearm. A large peacock, put on later to hide a nude woman, covers the other.

He is the first one to the gym every day. He leaves his apartment on Southwest 4th Street by midmorning, spends an hour in the corner drugstore having breakfast, and then takes two buses to get to Miami Beach by 10:30.

When Sully, the elfin, cigar-chomping curmudgeon, left the gym two years ago, Billy took over his job. He cleans up the place and collects the fighters' monthly dues and the spectators' fifty-cent admissions. Once he opens the front door at noon, he sits behind an old card table and signs in the fighters.

Billy grew up in Maine and turned to boxing as a teenager. By the time he retired from a career as a journeyman featherweight, he had had over one hundred professional bouts. Once he was in Willie Pep's stable. But ten years ago, he was down on his luck.

"I walked out of Maine dead broke," he said. "Until I got myself together I lived in flophouses and missions, always working my way south. One of the toughest times was when I was staying in a mission in Raleigh. I read that there was a fair near town and they wanted ex-boxers and wrestlers to fight a young gorilla.

"I figured I had been in with some of the best boxers in the world so I could hold my own with a gorilla. I had planned to dance, but the SOB ran out, banged me in the leg, flipped me tail end over teacup, and then started jumping up and down on my chest. He busted my ribs. I crawled out, got my ten dollars, and finally made my way to Miami.

"I worked with amateur boxers here, and after a while I ended up at the 5th Street Gym. There's nothing like this kind of atmosphere—the hustle and bustle, everybody trying to con everybody, laughter, friendship. You meet some fabulous characters in a boxing gym."

* * *

When Kid Chocolate, Moe Fleischer's fighter, first came to New York from Cuba, he had the habit of kneeling down in a corner and blessing himself just before the initial bell. It nearly put his career into an immediate dive.

"He was fighting this guy who was a real quick starter," said Fleischer. "I warned Chocolate the guy would come out fast, but before he got all the way up from praying the bell rang. This guy charged across the ring with a right hand that knocked him down.

"I thought this might be the end of his career, so I got up on the apron and reached into the ring. I had a capsule of smelling salts hidden in my hand. The ringside judge asked me what I was doing and I said I saw some cotton on the canvas that I didn't want Chocolate to trip over. I stuck the salts under his nose, and he beat the count. He didn't know where he was for five rounds, but he finally shook it off and managed a draw. It saved his career."

Fleischer became a match maker in 1944 and soon was known as one of the best in the business. He was running three clubs every week. He became known as "Sell-Out Moe" when he sold out the four thousand seats of Brooklyn's Ridgewood Grove for twenty-three straight Saturday nights. One of his last matches was the title fight between Floyd Patterson and Ingemar Johansson at Yankee Stadium.

"My wife, Lily, and I were married forty-seven years when she passed away in 1966," Fleischer said softly. "I was disgusted with everything after that. I was ready to go to pieces when Chris Dundee sent for me. We had known each other since the forties. He knew I knew my business, so he brought me in to help."

After he got here, Fleischer trained Bahamian Elijah Obed to the junior middleweight title of the world. Even at eighty, Fleischer stays active. He now works with unbeaten junior middleweight Kenny Whetstone.

"This has given me new life," he said. In the fifteen years he has been in Miami, he said he has come to the gym 7 days a week, 365 days a year. The only time he missed was a two-week period two years ago. He couldn't find a way to sneak out of the hospital.

Jerry White, an old fighter himself, ran his own gym on 6th Street from 1950 to 1962. He called his place the Magic City Gym, and it had its own colorful lot. Many of them hung out there for the knock rummy card games.

"We had the same guys every day," said White. "There was Evil Eye Finkle and Sam the Mumbler, Raincoat Rabinowitz and Tip Toe Tannenbaum, the house dick at one of the hotels. Mumbler used to put the cards up his sleeve, and when I'd clean up afterwards, I could find forty-six, maybe forty-seven cards."

His gym, he said, was the first that was integrated in the state. Because White had permitted black fighters to train at his place after a Coral Gables gym refused them, heavyweight Joe Louis held his workouts there when he came to Miami for his fight with Omelio Agramonte in the Orange Bowl.

"There was lots of action here, especially when I came down here to fight in the thirties," said White. "They had the Causeway Arena where the *Miami News* and *Herald* building now sets. And there were shows at the Million Dollar Pier at First Street on the Beach. Minsky held his burlesque shows there, too. Al Jolson was a regular at the fights."

Lou Gross, with his cigar, red-tinted glasses, and loud sports coat, was one of the more respected fight trainers in the country. Willie Pastrano and Carlos Ortiz won their titles with him in the corner. He claims he quit school and became the youngest fight manager in

Everyone celebrating Moe Fleischer's birthday. Dwaine Simpson Collection.

the country—at age fourteen. "I was big for my age," he said noncha-
lantly.

Now he writes a weekly boxing column for a Chicago entertainment
newspaper and a monthly piece for a paper in Broward County. Since
he lives in Fort Lauderdale and doesn't drive, it's a three-hour, four-bus
trip, one way to the gym each day. He explained his sixty years in the
game simply: "I starved in this business. I made money and now I'm
starving again."

Then there is Larry Golub, who worked for Coca-Cola in New York.
He used to come to Miami every year on his vacation. Each time he
visited, he worked the fight shows as a cutman. He doesn't make it to
the gym much anymore, because Rose, his wife of fifty-five years, is
very ill. Although he cares for her around the clock, he does manage to
slip over to the gym for an hour a couple of times a week.

"It's good for me," he said. "Not just the atmosphere, but the fight
game itself. I was making a living all my life, so it was never for the
money. It's just that I love this game and this gym lets me stay close
to it."

*   *   *

Two hours after they come to the gym, they all are gone. They slowly walk down the wooden steps, leaving the magical boxing world upstairs. Golub goes back to his ailing Rose, Gross goes off on another three-hour bus ride, Fleischer plods to his little hotel room down the street, and Sheridan heads back across the causeway to Miami.

By midafternoon, the 5th Street Gym is again empty. And then the sun dips behind the old hotel across the street and the gym cools off and the memories grow dim with another day.

My Memories of Chris Dundee

Bob Sheridan

Bob Sheridan is a jolly Rabelaisian radio blow-by-blow man. He holds the record for doing more championship bouts than anyone else in the history of radio. His call of the Rumble in the Jungle is the best example of a perfect call of a major fight. He is called the Colonel because at one time he was the head of the state police in Massachusetts.

It was 1963 and I was a sophomore at the University of Miami, a transplanted Bostonian playing baseball for the legendary coach Ron Fraser. The baseball scholarships were skimpy compared to the football scholarship, so Ron Fraser worked hard to find ways for us to make a buck or two during the off season.

A local promoter named Chris Dundee called the coach asking if he could send over some players to sell sodas at the fight that night. That didn't fit our egos too well, as we were star University of Miami players. "Yeah, and starving to death," said my more realistic roommate, Kenny Unger. You won't believe this, but when we got to Miami Beach, we find that we're to sell sodas for the first Liston-Ali fight. That was my introduction to the babbling, nonstop-moving character named Chris Dundee. He took us around and showed us where to sell the most sodas and not have to walk too far from the Coca-Cola stand. Kenny and I were like two rubes from a farm. The glamour of the crowd

The Colonel *(left)* with Ferdie. Luisita Sevilla Pacheco.

overwhelmed us. Then we began to feel the animal magnetism of a heavyweight title fight crowd.

By the time the fight started, I had picked up the pulse of the crowd. I, who had entered ignorant of the drama of Cassius Clay versus Sonny Liston, now openly rooted for the brash young mouthy kid to upset Liston. Kenny looked at me as if I'd gone crazy. "What do you know?" I smiled a big smile. "No, what do you know?" I said. Welcome to a major fight. God, it was so exciting. Clay was so big, bigger than Liston and faster, and he could box like a dream. Kenny jumped ship. "Changed my mind. The mouthy kid is going to win." We were on solid ground from round one to four, but then, disaster! Clay was blind in the corner. A little white guy was working like a madman, all the time talking, talking, and talking. "He's gonna quit," I shouted, my heart beating wildly. "He's going to quit!" "Not on Angelo Dundee, he ain't," said a tough guy behind me. He'd paid $150 for his ticket. Chris was like that. He worked us like slaves in a Siberian labor camp, then sat us in a ringside seat so we would always remember our first fight. Oh, baby, was he right about that!

Ali with the flag. Kurt Severin.

Now little Angelo was pulling the reluctant blinded Cassius up on his feet. The referee started over. Angelo punched Ali forward with an exhortation, "Run, baby, run!" And run he did. We watched with our heart in our mouth. They were right above us. For the first time, we felt the danger of the fight. One solid punch from Liston could turn the fight around, yet Cassius would not quit! He ran. "Run, run, run," we yelled at Clay, over and over as if our lives were at stake, not his.

We were being initiated into the breast of the beast, a fight crow, and when it roared, the foundation of the building rocked. I was hooked. Clay survived the round. The next round, Clay beat on Liston savagely. Clay won when Liston quit, and I found myself fighting to get close to Ali, to just touch him as he yelled to the reporters, "I told you! I told you, I shook up the whole wide world!" I wanted to be part of that Cassius Clay world. I wanted to stand with Angelo Dundee, Drew Bundini Brown, Dr. Ferdie Pacheco, and Luis Sarria to be a part of that. Somehow, to do something that would justify my being part of that. Big-time boxing.

Being blessed with a tremendous lack of ability to play baseball at a pro level, I found work in a 50,000–watt radio show. I was discovered by Ken Malden, who was the sports director. He asked if I knew Chris Dundee. "Hell, yes, I knew Chris. I was his guest at the Clay-Liston fight." Well, it was almost a truth. And that was what I was doing that first day at the gym.

I leaped at the chance to go to the mecca of boxing, but when I arrived I thought I was in the wrong place. The gym was a dump, on the second floor of a corner drugstore and an out-of-town newspapers stand. It was in a seedy section of South Beach (in those days all of South Beach was a dump, I just didn't know it).

Away I went up two flights of termite-ridden, rickety stairs to be greeted by a gnome of a guy with a cigar butt stuck in his toothless mouth. He asked for a quarter. Indignantly I said, "I'm press."

"Yeah, yeah. Press my pants. Let's see the coin, you mud toitle."

Suitably chastised, I produced a quarter. My first impression was that the old dump was a shit-hole. The seedy old place was filled with old ragged men with cigars stuck in their mouth. Among them floated beautiful animal figures, the boxers bending to their task. The old guys huddled by the ring, where two huge black guys were whaling the bejesus out of each other. Black cigar saliva trailed down their chins and stained their shorts. I picked out the youngest of the gray men, a man with a big paunch and balding, wearing the obligatory checkered polyester stretch pants three inches too short, white socks, and black shoes. It looked like a uniform of some kind. What set him off was a red corner man's sweater. Once, in another lifetime, up north in the long ago, a fighter had bought Lou Gross a sweater and put his name on it. The fighter lost. Lou kept the sweater and put white adhesive tape on the back. Even Lou Gross couldn't remember who the original fighter was. "He wuz a bum," Lou growled. To him everyone under the rank of champion was a bum. Every corner man except himself and Angelo were "shoemakers," amateurs. He was a boiling cauldron of acid criticism. People tolerated him because of his youth. He was sixty-seven.

"Chris? Over by the ring. On the phones. Ain'cha got eyes?" he said in response to my question, and I spun away, anxious to get away from his stinky cigar and evil disposition.

Dundee's desk was next to a sixteen-by-sixteen-foot ring, in a corner. He had two phones, one black and the other a bright red; this one had a lock on the dial. Chris was talking into both phones at the same time. Between an argument over money and a contract negotiation, Chris looked me over, searching his fabulous mind for my identification.

"You are the baseball player," he said, smiling a broad smile. "What you doing here? Don't tell me you want to be a fighter."

"I'm here to see if we can carry the Tuesday night fights on our radio show," I blurted out. Chris said good-bye at the same time and hung up the phones.

When Chris was getting good news, he paid exclusive attention. Rated coverage was definitely good news.

I couldn't shake my impression that Chris in perpetual motion was the guy behind the curtain in the *Wizard of Oz*. He couldn't seem to stop talking. I was a pretty good talker, and I got shut out.

Before we could agree on a deal, Chris had me looking at the names, weights, and records of all the undercard fighters. "oh," he said. "And the ring announcer is Frank Freeman." Chris paused. "If you get stuck, ask Frank. He knows everything and has the spiel of a shingle salesman, which is what he was." Whew! I caught my breath. Chris had me turned around and headed for the door before I could frame an answer.

"Now that I'm working for Chris, can I have my quarter back?"

"Get outta here, you mud toitle, you." The little guy looked like he might have a gun in the drawer. I fled.

On the street, in the pounding sunshine, my heart was bursting with joy.

"Oh, boy, I'm part of the 5th Street Gym. I'm inside boxing." I thought again. "Or I'm Dundee's PR man."

That auspicious start was in 1967, and from then till today I have broadcast on radio and television five thousand fights.

The next day I went to our prefight lunch, which I wish I'd recorded. We established a father-son relationship, this strange, Groucho Marx–like man and me. Until his death four decades later, I loved Chris Dundee like my own dad.

Chris Dundee introduced me to the full world of boxing. As I observed and studied this man, I learned it all: the hustle in boxing, the moves to make to fix a judge, how to influence a negative writer, how to match fighters. I met all the crusty, spidery old gray men of the 5th Street Gym. This ghostly brigade of skeletal old fellows took me in and told me their secrets of long-ago "fixes" and "dumperinos." They talked about a title fight that had taken place thirty years before 1910 as if it were yesterday. To them, it *was* yesterday.

His introduction of me as one of the 5th Street Gym inner circle made me accepted instantly by Ali, Luis Manuel Rodriguez, Willie Pastrano, Florentino Fernandez, Gomeo Brenan, and any old-timer to come by, like Joe Louis or Sugar Ray Robinson. I was in heaven. My microphone was my passport. Boy, I wish I could have kept those tapes!

As I became well known, Chris Dundee would take me on road trips. There was nothing in the world like traveling with Chris, Angelo, and the entourage. The best way to describe a single thing like picking up your luggage upon arrival in any city was like something of the Three Stooges and the Marx Brothers combined. Customs officers hated to see us arrive. The only difference was that those guys were trying to be funny; our guys weren't trying to be funny, they just were. They lived funny.

Years went by in a blaze of fights and fun. I was asked by Chris to cover the Al Blue Lewis versus Muhammad Ali fight in Dublin, Ireland. My flight was late, and I just got to the outside of Croke Park. I had no ticket, no credentials, just my tape recorder. I stood on the curb watch-

Sheridan with staff. *Left to right*: Sis Haiflex, Bob Sheridan, Pancho Limon, and ring card girl. Luisita Sevilla Pacheco.

ing the big shots come in. Suddenly Chris, in a limo, opened the door and pulled me in. "Stick close to me," he said. We hid in Ali's dressing room, where I got a mountain of good stuff from Ali, Angelo, and Ferdie. When it came time to go out, Chris again grabbed me. "Stick close to me," he said. When we arrived at ringside, Chris got his chair and we shared it—almost but not quite. Both of us have huge bottoms, so we struggled to remain seated. I set up my broadcast position. It was primitive, but it worked. We were live to Miami.

We got up close. By up close, I mean we were right in Ali's corner, and we could pick up all the corner chatter. It was super radio. But Chris was more than half deaf at the time, and he kept talking to me, asking questions. I can't figure out to this day what Chris thought I was doing, but I repeatedly had to keep saying, "Shut the fuck up while I call this fight!"

The trips home were classics. People fought not to sit by Chris. Going on an airliner was roughly like going camping. Chris brought pillows, blankets, and puffy slippers.

He carried more than thirty newspapers in his briefcase. All covered the fight. Only about 20 percent were in English. I would try to sleep, and Chris would wake me and make me read the column. I would fake it, and soon he would ask what I thought.

Chris Dundee was a trip all in himself. He was funny as hell. A gregarious chatterbox, he would have the entire cabin conscripted to boxing by the time we landed. Chris Dundee was one of a kind. I was privileged to share his life for four decades. His influence in the sport of boxing was universal. He's in the Hall of Fame. Aside from boxing (and including Don King), Chris is easily the best- and most-loved character I've ever met in my life.

Colonel Bob Sheridan: The Irish Whirlwind

Ferdie Pacheco

For years, Bob Sheridan was a regular at the 5th Street Gym. I gravitated to his side purely because he was such a fascinating character and a laugh machine. Everything was funny to him. We shared a love of Chris Dundee, and Bob collected Dundee-isms. My kind of guy: a *storyteller.*

Once I started to keep a log of all of his crazy adventures. After a few years, I showed the work to a literary agent and to a theatrical agent. Everyone I showed it to said, "This is hilarious. But it's fiction, right? There's no one like the Colonel, is there? If he's real, *no one* will believe these stories."

There you have it—too big a figure to be real. Exhausted, I quit taking notes.

Now, at the end of our lives, I am amazed that no one has recorded his journey through the boxing scene. I am not going to do a book. I can't sell it. What I can do is a random search through the nuttiness and fun of the Colonel's life. It's random, so don't look for order or a time frame, because I can't remember and neither can he. Fasten your safety belts; here is a bit, a chunk, of what life with the Colonel was like on the highway of boxing.

The Colonel is from a big Irish family from Boston. Boston. That's *Irish*. As in, Irish pub, Irish bar, and Irish blarney.

The Colonel always worked in radio. That is to say, he had a voice. People loved his wide-open, brawling, funny style. If he was on the right side of a politician, the politician was guaranteed to be elected. Sheridan's voice counted in Boston.

So it was that he backed a mildly crooked Irish politician for mayor and his pal for governor. Both got elected, and Sheridan was in the tall cotton. They searched for a way to reward Bob. They decided to make him a Colonel of the state police. With no experience, Bob found himself *boss* of the state police. The opposition howled, "He has no qualifications!" The response was, "Neither did Bobby Kennedy, yet his brother appointed him to be attorney general." Irish politics are inter-mingled with rationalizations like that. It's like being a part of a wild Irish family.

For a few years, Sheridan was in every parade and at every state function. He had a resplendent uniform made with two oversized ea-gles on his shoulders. He didn't do much, but everywhere he went, he had a presence: when you saw Colonel Sheridan, you saw the State of Massachusetts.

The mayor warned Bob, "Don't make bets on the limo phone. Don't talk about fixed home races . . . or a fixed fight."

"What's the use of the phone, then?" asked the irrepressible Colo-nel.

Eventually, his blatant disregard for the law and his abuse of power as the head of the state police got him sacked. He pushed off a few steps ahead of the posse and headed for Vegas, where his shenanigans were admired. There he found his niche as the blow-by-blow TV-radio announcer for Don King fights.

Understand something right here, before we continue with anec-dotes of his zany life. We've been in boxing together for forty years. I know his work. Let me state categorically:

Bob Sheridan is the best blow-by-blow announcer ever in the his-tory of broadcast fights. He has broadcast over 850 title fights. No one else comes close. If you want to teach a class on calling fights, put on your DVD of *The Rumble in the Jungle,* Ali versus Foreman. Sheridan's call is brilliant. You just can't do it better. Every week, Sheridan doesn't miss doing the fight, and his call is always the best.

His work ethic is beyond comparison. Consider this: we were at the Tyson-Holyfield fight (and it was almost as big as Ali-Frazier). We got word that Sheridan had had a heart attack and wouldn't be able to make it to the fight. I felt sad. A big fight without Bob Sheridan at ringside? It didn't seem real.

Suddenly, during the prelim, I heard a commotion at the rear of the building. In came a wheelchair with all kinds of I.V. tubes and oxygen hoses. Sitting up and smiling like a Roman consul, there was the King of the Communicators, Bob Sheridan, waving at his disbelieving colleagues in the packed press section. Behind him he had two cardiologists and two emergency squad nurses. I couldn't believe my eyes.

"O.K., me boy-o. I'm in place. Let's get the show on the road." His smile was wide. The Colonel was enjoying his entrance!

I left my broadcast position and went over to give him a giant hug.

"I just want to warn you, Colonel, if you fall over in the middle of the fight, don't look for me to give you mouth to mouth, you disgusting Irish sprite."

He laughed uproariously, reached back and grabbed a comely nurse by the arm, and brought her into the conversation.

"That's what I've got her here for, me boy-o." The nurse turned red and twittered. The doctor and nurses were enjoying being part of the Sheridan bandwagon. They were worried that Sheridan couldn't take the excitement, but Sheridan was the only man not worried for his life.

He stood up at the broadcast position, faced the crowd, lifted his two arms, and yelled, "If he dies, he dies!" And a roar of laughter from his press buddies greeted him. Sheridan loved this.

Sheridan was back! He would not miss a great fight. It was one more night on his long record. He would die later.

I kept an eye on him. Above us, Mike Tyson was getting his ass kicked by Evander Holyfield. Beside me, the Colonel was winning his fight for his life, and he was doing a helluva job on the fight. What a guy!

Suddenly, an unbelievable event occurred: Tyson bit the top of Holyfield's ear off. The piece of the ear bounced off the canvas right to me! I considered taking it and tossing it to Sheridan, but the ref was asking for it. Sheridan, red in the face, was in heaven. This was what he risked his life for! If he was crazy to come, it's because he knows boxing is a crazy event. Anything can and does happen. Isn't that worth dying for? I ask you.

Well, enough of Sheridan, the best blow-by-blow announcer that has ever lived. I've got to get in a few "Sheridan-isms" to give you the feel of what life around Sheridan is like.

We were in Paris for an *NBC Sports World* show. I was out with a camera crew looking for a gag to introduce the show with. So far, we'd struck out. Sheridan had a table right on the sidewalk where a parade of tourists was promenading. It was only one in the afternoon, and the lunch bunch was out walking. Sheridan had ordered *six* cognacs at one time. He lined them up. He was in his prime. He had that gleam in his eye which meant to me that he was up to some Irish mischief.

A dandified Parisian gentleman was walking a tiny furry animal on a leash with many rhinestones attached. He smelled of perfume. "What a beautiful dug," Irish Bob said in a phony French accent, like Inspector Clouseau. "Merci," sniffed the snob, horrified to be addressed by this American acting like a Frenchman. "Where is his *bun?*" asked Sheridan, mispronouncing the word *bone,* as the inspector does. "What did you say?" the insulted Frenchman asked, drawing himself up to his full height.

Sheridan pushed back his chair and drew himself to his full height, which is around six feet tall. He asked, "Where is his bun? Don't you have a B-U-N for your doggie?"

"Impertinent American tourist!" said the Frenchman. Then he made a mistake. He drew back his fist as if to hit Bob. Bob ducked under the punch and came back with a hook to the man's liver. He folded over. Bob then threw a gigantic uppercut, right on the chin. Down went the Frenchman, flat on his back. He groaned and rolled over on his face. Blood oozed from his nose.

Bob grabbed a bread stick and used it like a broadcast mike:

"The Frenchman is down—one, two, three, he's on his face, this does not look good, ladies and gentlemen—six, seven, he's not getting up, and he is leaking blood from his nose. No, ladies and gentlemen, he is *not* getting up—eight, nine, ten, he's *out*. The winner is Irish Bob Sheridan."

Then we paid the bill and ran down the street before the gendarmes came to drag the Colonel to the Bastille.

"Did you get the knockout on camera?" he asked our amazed cameraman, a twenty-one-year-old youth from New York. "That was a fine piece of work," I said to him. He beamed. "Stick with the Colonel. We *create* the news."

The Colonel has always been a ladies' man. For a while now, he has been a happily married man. He is a stay-at-home husband in Vegas. But outside of Vegas before he was married . . . the Beast was unchained and he sought out company, usually of the paying kind. His adventures were varied.

In Houston, after a Sugar Ray Leonard fight, he was at the bar doing serious damage to a bottle of J&B Scotch. There was a dearth of feminine company. The bartender made a call.

In walked a statuesque beauty with a marked resemblance to Jane Russell. The Aussie news guys started lining up to buy her drinks. At the end of the bar lay the Beast, regarding the girl like a lion regards a lamb. He will wait until she is "ripe," then he'll move in and "close the deal."

"Closing time," said the bartender, ringing a big cowbell. The Colonel swooped down and made his move.

"Let's get a fresh bottle and go to my room. I've got some Glenn Miller sides and a C note."

We were in a Quadrangle Motel with a patio in the middle. It had two floors, and Sheridan's room was on the second floor. We settled down to drink in the patio to await Sheridan's stories of his tryst with Jane Russell.

Upstairs, they were drinking J&B out of water glasses. The Colonel put on some sweet Glenn Miller—"At Last" and "The Moonlight Serenade"—and they got up to dance.

The first thing that came off was the tops: shirts and undershirts flew, joined by the blouse and bra. She *was* Jane Russell. The Colonel took full advantage of the giant mammaries, and they kissed passionately. Tongues flew into every orifice available. Bob was as hot as a cheap pistol. He unzipped his fly, pulled off his BVD's, and unleashed his monster.

She did the same! Bob blinked. Could it be that he was looking at a large, erect Texas penis? He roared with savage indignation, "Why, you are a . . . guy!" "What difference does that make?" he/she replied provocatively, hands on hips, his penis waving in the breeze. "I can do anything a women can do," he/she said, standing by the window so the outside lights played on his large, throbbing, erect penis. The sight horrified the Colonel.

"*Try flying!*" said the irate Colonel, and he threw him/her out of the second-story window. She/he flew, arms spread as though in a swan dive and the erect penis acting like a rudder, right into a cactus plant.

"Cor-blimey," said an Aussie heading for the car, "I think we'd best take off."

The Colonel took back his $100 bill, walked majestically to his car, and sped off into the Texas night.

Finding himself in need of an emotional uplift (the Colonel did not know how to spell or define *depression*), he went to Vegas, sat at a table with a row of drinks, and proceeded to play until unconsciousness dictated that be taken to his room.

He awoke at noon with a super headache and a sense of doom. He had not one penny in his jeans. This was not a new sensation for the Colonel, though. He had his plane fare back to Miami, and anyone would float him a hundred bucks for last-minute play at the tables and a free lunch.

The phone rang.

"Colonel, sir, this is bookkeeping. When can you come down to settle up?"

Uh-oh. The moment had come.

"How much is it?" asked Bob, hoping for a reasonable figure.

"Fifty thousand, sir."

"What?" Bob jumped out of bed.

"Fifty thousand dollars. Do you want a check, or cash, or should we wire it to your bank?"

Bob sat down with a thud.

"Cash will do," he said and restrained an impulse to cancel his Miami flight, back to the real world, where he knew that the 5th Street Gym did not have slot machines.

I must pause here to briefly outline what the Colonel's life was like in his playboy mid-years. Nobody had more fun than the Colonel.

The Colonel was a reckless and driven gambler; his biggest danger was to do a fight in Vegas. Between hookers and gambling, the Colonel would come back to Miami dead broke and with his tail between his legs. He would smile and start again.

During the happy-go-lucky time, he fooled us all by leaving his sports commentary TV-radio job and going into bull riding in the rodeo! What qualifications or talents he had for the dangerous sport of bull riding no one knew, and Bob didn't explain.

Before you can say "Yippie-kai-yo!" the Colonel was a champion bull rider and earning big money. One night at a huge rally in Madison Square Garden, Bob faced a particularly nasty bull which apparently had an aversion to sportscasters. The bull threw the Colonel high in the sky, and he landed on his back upon the barrier. The Colonel went straight to the hospital with a broken back. That appeared to be the end of his relationship with cattle, but that was not to be, as we shall see.

Now, Colonel Sheridan is an Irish patriot. Bob took the $50,000 and bought a farm in Ireland. It bred cattle and bulls. Because of his connection with bull riding, this did not seem suspicious to the authorities. Bob's expansive personality soon made him the most popular man in the county. He could have run for mayor and been elected in a landslide. So you might well ask, what the hell did *that* have to do with being an Irish patriot?

Well, Bob bought cattle in Texas and shipped them to himself by air. The cargo planes had a false bottom, which held the fecal output of the cattle. Nobody in his right mind would examine the second section. It was there that he stashed weapons and ammo for the Irish Republican

Army, the IRA. No one ever caught on. This went on for several years, and Bob made a lot of money.

Bob went entirely overboard about this Irish business, and he finally succumbed to the idea of settling down on his comfortable Irish farm. He decided to marry an Irish girl, a registered nurse and straightlaced Catholic. Clearly, she was out of his league.

They stayed married for a few years, but soon the battles inside their house were much worse than the battles in the streets with the British army. It all came tumbling down, and they moved back to the States only a few steps ahead of the police.

Flash forward a few years, to after a bitter and costly divorce. Bob had suffered one of his four heart attacks. He was in a New York hospital. It was dark. Bob was in pain. He needed a Demerol shot desperately. He rang for the nurse. He was delirious. The flashlight of the night nurse illuminated his arm to give a shot, and he heard a familiar voice:

"I could stick this needle to the bone!"

Yikes! It was the voice of his ex-wife and sworn enemy. Bob yelled out, weakly, "Help! I need a nurse!" and passed out. Nothing is ever easy with Bob.

Bob's hospital stays were legendary because of his inability to take things seriously.

The Colonel was in intensive care, just barely out of critical condition, his outcome still in doubt. He was allowed one visit per afternoon. A line of friends waited for the chance to see him. One of his best friends since they were lads was an Italian kid, Balducci (not his real name), who owned a string of funeral parlors. Since they were small, they had played what they called the Movie Game. That was predicated on picking out famous sayings from the movies. For example, Bogart to Ingrid Bergman in *Casablanca:* "Here's looking at you, kid!" They had hundreds by the time they grew up and went their separate ways.

The cardiac physician's grand rounds came to Bob's bed, and the consultation was serious. Bob saw Balducci. "Balducci, my oldest buddy! I been waiting for you!"

The doctor, thinking that Balducci was coming to arrange for Bob's funeral, had to reassure Bob that he was nowhere near needing Balducci's funeral parlor.

Bob leaned forward in bed and in a relieved tone said, "Thank God you've come." Cough, cough. "The gold is in the . . ." and he slumped over. Balducci caught him before he fell out of bed.

"Condition red!" The medical team yelled. Every doctor and nurse went into action.

Bob smiled and hugged Balducci.

Bob is in his seventies now, still at ringside, still clearly the best blow-by-blow announcer in the business. Bob has a small, highly efficient unit, and no one messes with them. They ask for no help; they set up, do a great show, pack up, and go home. That is the way it should be done. Not even Don King bothers him. King pays him well and leaves him alone to call the fight as he sees it. Bob and Don King love each other but stay out of each other's way.

The last thing I have to say about the Colonel is that I regret not being able to do boxing shows together. I think we would have set a record for being the best in boxing. Two highly knowledgeable boxing men who are great storytellers. What a combination!

Once, by chance, we did work together. We went to Peking for Showtime to do a Laila Ali fight. I *never* work a women's boxing fight. I am dead set against women's boxing, but Laila Ali is Muhammad Ali's daughter, and (by coincidence) I happened to *deliver* her, so I felt a little responsible. Besides which, she was a huge attraction for the Chinese press. I looked out my hotel window and there was a nine-story cutout of Laila! Wow!

Boxing on Showtime had slowly degenerated from a mediocre mess to an absolute mess as the two guys who ran the show started to take over the show. They wrote everything that the announcer, Steve Albert, had to say. They *tried* to write mine, too, but I spurned their orders. Nobody can *write* what I *think*. I was at war with these two mediocrities when Bob Sheridan came into the picture.

Steve Albert's father had died. We got to Peking and he got the news, turned around, and went home to be with his grieving family. What a killer that was.

I suggested that we use Bob Sheridan, who fit in with me so well. They had no other recourse, so they said yes.

Bob has never done network TV. He is used to being the authoritative voice of the program. He takes no orders, doesn't allow for suggestions, and just does his usual clean show.

Almost immediately, we banged heads with the two mediocrities about the opening. They would write what the Colonel would say, what he was thinking, though I would say whatever I wanted. They tried hard to get Bob to read the cue cards, but at airtime Bob threw away the cue cards and winged it as he always does. He fit in perfectly with me, and we jokingly ad-libbed a funny opening segment.

Me: "Bob, do you realize that you and I have worked title fights on every continent in the world?"

Bob (with a blank face): "Not Antarctica."

Me: "Now, don't tell me you did a fight from Antarctica?"

Bob: "Yep. On an aircraft carrier."

Me: "Oh."

And so it went, bumping heads all during the telecast. Here's an example:

When the bell rang ending the round, the TV cameras followed one fighter into his corner. At that point, Bob said, "And so we follow boxer A to his corner. Let's listen in . . ." And we hear the corner men working.

We had an officious, over-his-head producer who had a huge racial chip on his shoulder. The son of the discredited New York mayor David Dinkins, he couldn't sort out whether he was black or white. He knew nothing of boxing and less of televising it. He had, out of the blue, plucked the idea that we should *not* say that we were going into the corner; we should remain silent. I looked at Bob, and I knew he wasn't about to listen to Dinkins's orders.

Bob: "Let's follow the fighter to his corner . . ."

Voice on the intercom, an enraged Dinkins: "Goddamnit! Don't you *ever* say that again on *this* fucking telecast!"

A pause . . . Bob slowly pushed his button and in a Clint Eastwood whisper full of menace said, "I hope you weren't talking to me!"

Silence in the truck. We finished the show and did it all *our way*. It was a great show.

The producers and vice presidents made a note: never put Sheridan and Pacheco together again.

Well, I feel better now that I got some of the Colonel's colorful life in print. I hope a publisher sees this and offers him a book deal to do his book. It would be a best seller and could make a great movie or TV series—and if not, so what? Bob will go on doing his excellent call at ringside. After all, he knows where the gold is buried.

The Life and Times of Luis Sarria

Enrique Encinosa

Enrique Encinosa is an unusual member of the Cuban boxing world. He is intelligent and an acute observer. He boxed a bit. At the amateur level he had 35 fights in Chicago and Indiana when he was in high school and college, trained by former bantamweight champion Johnny Coulton. He trained fighters, he worked in corners in Miami. He wrote knowledgeable books on the history of Cuban fighters and did radio and TV commentary on fights. Enrique divided his time between his love for Cuban fighters, including Luis Manuel Rodriguez, Floro Fernandez, Douglas Vaillant, and the Miami-born Cuban Frankie Otero. Enrique is currently completing an extensive history of Cuban boxers, which will be the only large serious study of this part of Cuban history.

Sports historians enthralled with the Ali legend have written little about Luis Sarria. There are reasons for such apathy. Sarria knew little English, and his well-mannered, soft voice and quiet demeanor were overshadowed by the ranting of Bundini, the brilliant glibness of Pacheco, and the blue-collar appeal of Angelo Dundee.

The sports historians missed out on a treasure find. Luis was one of the most interesting characters in the game, considered among Cubans to be the greatest fight trainer the nation ever produced. He had wit and a dignified manner that was the mirror of his good soul.

Luis Sarria was born on the 29th of October, 1911, in Cumanayagua, a farming town in central Cuba. His childhood was marked by poverty, hunger, illness, and death. One of his sisters died before reaching adulthood. A brother—with whom Luis shared a bed—died in his sleep. By the age of twelve, Sarria was an orphan who wore hand-me-down clothes and had known gnawing hunger in his belly.

Many years later, when a journalist made a casual remark about having skipped lunch and feeling very hungry, Sarria smiled and said softly, "You don't know what going hungry is like. Son, when you are hungry you can eat melted lead."

He was on his own by the age of thirteen, working at shining shoes in a street stall in the southern city of Cienfuegos. As he grew in size and strength, he made good wages for very hard work during the season of the sugar harvest, wielding a sharp machete under the hot Cuban sun. He also worked in the tobacco fields of Las Villas Province, in central Cuba.

Luis Sarria started boxing at the age of thirteen, fighting in amateur smokers where a hat would be passed for the fighters and winning bettors would tip their favorites. After a few fights—mostly victories—Sarria turned pro, beating an American fighter named Ernie Balin in a four-round fight.

"The money was not there," he said about his prelim fights. "They paid a peso a round, so it was four pesos for a four-rounder. That was very little money, but when I did not have any money at all, a peso could buy me a couple of cheap meals to get by another day."

Sarria fought in Cienfuegos and Santa Clara, winning most of his bouts, then headed for Havana, a very active fight center, where he set up a shoe-shine stand in the porch of a café named El Polo. He lived in a cheap boardinghouse and trained at a boxing gym to earn a few bucks after working a full shift.

Sarria shined shoes and sold newspapers, fighting prelim bouts for a few pesos. He scored a win over Pedro Canales and was a known undercard fighter at Cuba's famed Arena Cristal, a venue that had featured Kid Chocolate as one of its headline performers.

For his first main event in 1938, Sarria was paid fifty pesos. His opponent was Ramon Rodriguez, an established journeyman welterweight with a decent punch and a difficult southpaw style. "It was the toughest fight of my life," Sarria recalled in a rare interview, many years later.

"He hit very hard, dropping me early, but by then I knew how to survive, and it took all my skill to last the ten rounds, losing on points."

Sarria realized that his career as a boxer was going nowhere. He was a good boxer with a fighting heart, but he lacked power and his chin was ordinary. His last fight took place in 1939, when he faced Domingo Govin, a young welterweight with a hungry attitude. In the first round, both men threw hard right hands and went down in a rare double knockdown. Both lifted themselves groggily from the canvas, but Sarria was the worst of the two as their seconds worked over them in their corners.

"I lost by a TKO in two," Sarria said. "Referee Benitez stepped in, and that was my last, my thirtieth pro fight. I won nineteen."

Luis Sarria continued to shine shoes but began a new career as a boxing trainer. A pattern was soon established: Sarria's fighters won most of their fights. The young trainer did not allow his students to climb through the ropes unfit, nor did he overmatch them to make a quick buck. Green kids became proficient inside the ropes, and his amateur team picked up medals at tournaments.

By 1943, Luis Sarria had become the trainer in the corner for the legendary Kid Tunero, an old Cuban pro who defeated four world titleholders, including Ezzard Charles. In 1948, Sarria was named trainer for the Cuban amateur team, winning three gold medals at the Guatemala Central American Games.

The 1950s established Luis Sarria as one of Cuba's best trainers. He was the teacher and corner for three future world champions: Luis Manuel Rodriguez, Sugar Ramos, and Jose Legra.

Sarria also worked with world contenders, including his amateur star–turned–pro heavyweight Julio Mederos, Spanish welterweight champion Ben Buker, lightweight Douglas Vaillant, and national flyweight titleholder Amado Mir.

Life was good. Luis was a respected trainer making a modest living, keeping his belly full while working at his favorite trade. His world changed in 1959 when Fidel Castro took power in Cuba. As Cuba entered into a civil war, with guerrilla fighting and resistance movements opposing the Marxist revolution and thousands being executed by firing squads, Luis Sarria contemplated leaving his country to live in a foreign land.

"Luis Manuel Rodriguez and I came to exile together," Sarria said in an interview.

When Castro took over Cuba he abolished pro boxing but it took him a couple of years to get around to doing it and boxers were allowed to fight in other countries. Luis Manuel Rodriguez and I traveled to the United States several times. Once, after a fight, we were both alone in the dressing room and I told him, "You go back alone this time." Luis Manuel looked at me and said, "Sarria, are you staying?" And I said to him, "Yes, I cannot go back to that crap." Luis Manuel looked at me and he nodded and then said, "I am staying also. I feel the same way."

In Miami, Sarria started life once again. He was flat broke, an exile in a strange land, but he had a good reputation as an honest trainer, and he had a friend in Angelo Dundee.

The Dundee brothers had spent over a decade importing and exporting Cuban fighters for their Miami Beach cards. Angelo spoke chopped-up Spanish, and his gym was filling up with new exiles: Luis Manuel Rodriguez, Florentino Fernandez, Jose Napoles, Angel Robinson Garcia, Sugar Ramos, Jose Legra, Douglas Vaillant, Johnny Sarduy, and a dozen other top talents.

Sarria became Angelo's right-hand man at the 5th Street Gym. He worked with prelim fighters and future champions as a second to Angelo and on the road with the journeyman pugs and contenders. Muhammad Ali was then Cassius Clay—a brash youth who idolized and studied Luis Manuel Rodriguez in the gym, watching the Cuban welterweight and copying some of his moves.

"I was training Luis," Sarria said. "And Ali spoke to me, but I do not speak English. Then he spoke to Angelo and he told me Ali wanted me to massage him. Our friendship started that day."

Sarria's big hands kneaded Ali's muscles. The Cuban trainer was not licensed as a masseur, but decades of gym work had taught him where every pinched nerve could be softened, how to break down the body fat, how to release tension. His large hands did their magic on

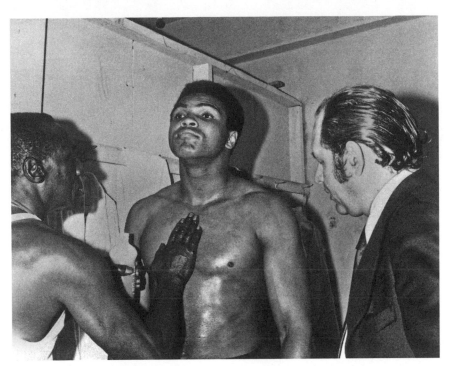
Ali with Luis Sarria *(left)* and Ferdie. Kurt Severin.

the fighter from Louisville, and Ali understood that the soft-spoken Cuban was in a league of his own.

Sarria learned only a few phrases of English and Ali could say few words in Spanish, but their language differences did not prevent both men from becoming friends, using their own sign language to communicate. Sarria became Ali's conditioner, training the Great One, running him through endless hours of sit-ups and knee bends, tuning his body while Dundee prepared the strategy for the upcoming bouts.

"The Ali years were unbelievable," Sarria said. "I worked with him for all but two of his title fights. I was there from beginning to end. Ali treated me well. He gave me a down payment for my house and paid me a good salary, but many people around him were leeches. Angelo and the sparring partners earned their money, but there were many in the camp that earned high salaries and did absolutely nothing. . . . Few cared for him as a human being."

The 1960s and early 1970s were the best years of Sarria's life. He traveled the planet with Ali, Willie Pastrano, Jimmy Ellis, Luis Manuel

Rodriguez, and a squad of top talent that included top-rated middle-weight Florentino Fernandez and lightweight contenders Douglas Vaillant and Frankie Otero.

He met presidents, kings, celebrities—including the Beatles—and intellectuals including Norman Mailer and Budd Schulberg. Sarria ate at the finest restaurants in Europe and the Orient and bunked at excellent hotels in all corners of the globe.

The shoe-shine prelim boy from Cumanayagua became a celebrity himself, being photographed and filmed as he worked in the gym with the Great One or stood at the corner of contenders and champions. He rode in motorcar parades in Africa, walked the ancient streets of Rome, visited the presidential mansion in Manila, felt the snow under his boots in Toronto, visited the Statue of Liberty in New York, gazed upon movie sets in Hollywood, and swam the beaches of Puerto Rico, the Bahamas, and Florida.

He was there—at the corner of the ring with Angelo and Ferdie—when Ali fought Joe Frazier, George Foreman, George Chuvalo, Ken Norton, and Leon Spinks. Sarria was there when Rodriguez faced George Benton, Rocky Rivero, Rubin Carter, Curtis Cokes, and Emile Griffith, when Frankie Otero traded leather with Ken Buchanan, and when Florentino Fernandez landed big left hooks on opponents' chins. Sarria once said,

> It was incredible. . . . I have a lot of tremendous memories. . . . In Manila it was exciting. In the middle rounds Frazier hurt Ali very bad and he was in pain. . . . Working the corner was a lot of pressure in that fight but Angelo is very smart at working a corner. . . . I first met Angelo in the fifties when he went to Cuba almost every week for the fights. . . . He was not rich or famous then. Like most trainers he was barely making a living.

One of the sad days of his career came when Luis Manuel Rodriguez lost a title bid to Nino Benvenuti. "Luis Manuel was a great fighter," Sarria said, "one of the greatest I ever saw, but he was shop-worn from more than a hundred fights, yet he gave the Italian a boxing lesson until Benvenuti threw that left hook. That was the hardest punch that

Ernesto Corral and Luis Sarria carry Luis Manuel after he wins the title. Enrique Encinosa Collection.

man ever threw. It caught Luis Manuel on the side of the jaw. When I saw Luis Manuel go down, I knew he wasn't going to stand up that time."

In the 1980s, Sarria contemplated retirement. He had a home, a family and several dogs, and a Social Security pension and Medicare, but he needed the fight game to stay alive, to feel useful. By then, the 5th Street Gym was too far to travel for an old trainer with increasing arthritis. He needed a place closer to his North Miami home.

Besides, the 5th Street Gym had changed. Ali and the top guns of the 1960s and 1970s had retired, melting back into civilian life. Angelo was still active but had moved his base of operations away from Miami Beach. Ferdie Pacheco was doing TV commentary for big fights and writing books. Chris Dundee was still active with sporadic promotions

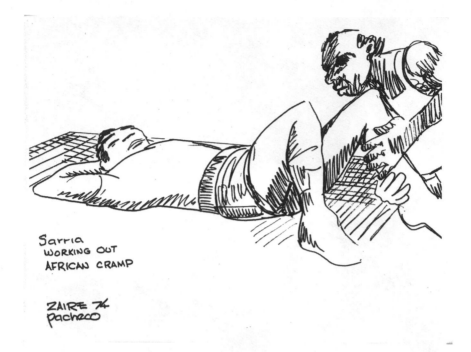

Sarria
WORKING OUT
AFRICAN CRAMP

ZAIRE 74
Pacheco

and booking some fighters, but the aging Chris no longer produced the weekly fight shows that had made the gym the bubbling cauldron of pugilistic activity of its heyday.

Enter Caron Gonzalez, an old friend from the time Sarria was a prelim pug. Caron was a muscular black man who had been a sparring partner of Kid Tunero and had become a very good trainer after an unspectacular and brief pro career as a welterweight. Caron had worked with Benny Paret and Jose Stable and was a very good teacher of infighting. Gonzalez was opening up a gym in Miami's Allapatah neighborhood—only a block away from where former welterweight champion Jack Britton had owned a drugstore—and Sarria was offered a chance to earn a few bucks and stay busy.

Caron and Sarria ran the gym for several years. Roberto Duran trained there for the "No mas!" fiasco with Sugar Ray Leonard, as did other champions including Happy Lora and Wilfredo Vazquez. Gonzalez and Sarria kept busy working with fighters like Puerto Rican lightweight Juan Arroyo, Cuban lightweight Pedro Laza, and a small army of prelim fighters hailing from all corners of the Caribbean. Sarria trained fighters, massaged bodies, and worked corners.

He would pace himself, taking breaks in which he sat ringside, puffing on a pipe, waiting for the arthritis to ease so he could stand again, to continue teaching the nuances of the jab or hook. Eventually, he stopped working corners, for it hurt too much to climb the few steps into the ring.

That was the beginning of the end of the Sarria story. All good things pass, and so do good men. Luis Sarria is no longer among us, but those who knew him will never forget his big smile, his large hands, his soft manners, and his bearing that Ferdie Pacheco equated with "the dignity of an African prince."

Not bad for a poor shoe-shine boy from Cumanayagua.

19

Sparring Partners

Willie Johnson

The sparring partner is a rare breed. He is defined as a boxer of moderate talents who deludes himself into thinking that one day he will be discovered in the gym, will be given a chance at a title, and will amazingly upset the champion and win a world championship.

The dream never changes. They trudge on, taking their daily beatings, wrapped in self-delusion while accepting the aches and pains. They return patiently to wait for their chance, and for most it never comes. But like gladiators in ancient Rome, they never think of their quest as hopeless. With a gleam in their eye, they point to Ali.

"Look at his sparring partners," they say: Larry Holmes, Jimmy Ellis, and Michael Dokes. All three were sparring partners. All three made it to the heavyweight championship of the whole, wide world. "Why not me? I sparred with Ali and Jimmy Ellis, too. See dat? I could be a champ." This was Willie's mantra.

Chris Dundee loved Willie as a father loves a devilish, mischievous son. Willie was always in trouble, but the cops who caught him in small crimes always let him go. They all loved him. He was always involved in nonviolent crimes and always with a girl, one of his "hos." Oh, he would steal their water, or take all their money after a busy night, but he wasn't a *criminal*.

"Ah, you know, officer. It's matrimonial." He would give the officer a laugh and his million-dollar smile. Willie had teeth—"teefus," he would call them—that belonged in the Dental Hall of Fame. He brushed four times a day but scorned floss and dentists who advocated it.

When a dentist who told him he would lose his teeth by the time he reached forty, he laughed, put his huge arm around the dentist's shoulder, and said, "Doc, with the chance I got to reach forty, I'll tell you what. If I get to forty, I'll floss four times a day."

"You're probably right," said the dentist.

The entire Overtown ghetto loved Willie. He was a kind of "bad boy" legend. I never met a girl who didn't care for Willie. He had the sweetest smile and a smooth jive manner. Girls just naturally loved to be wooed by Willie.

In my office, he was the most reliable patient. He was in for his penicillin shot to cure gonorrhea at least once a week, usually Monday after a long weekend debauch. Ms. Mabel, my upright pillar of the Church of Nurses, would cluck like a hen.

"Here *he* is again, Doctor. Why don't you turn him out to the Sanitation Department? He is a mess. A no-count, signifying *nigger* is what he is."

Willie would smile and try to put his arm around the righteous Ms. Mabel, who was steaming mad. I knew because she infrequently used the "n-word," unless the case warranted it. Once I admonished her, and she harrumphed. "Well, that's what he is—a *nigger.*" "Oh, my," I said.

One day, one of Willie's pals in sin came by for his ten-shot penicillin cure for syphilis. On the fifth day, he developed an allergy to penicillin, went into anaphylactic shock, and dropped dead at Ms. Mabel's feet.

"There's your lesson, Willie," she said when Willie came around to pick up the body. "You next? Keep on coming around for syphilis cure and *you next!*"

This shocked Willie so badly that he reformed his habits. He became so selective that one day he came by for a blood test. The death of his friend affected him so much that he started to go to Ms. Mabel's church. As it happened, the entire choir fell for his jiving. Willie, in a wild turnabout, picked the lead singer, who sounded like Mahalia Jackson but looked like Sonny Liston.

Willie shocked the neighborhood and married the girl. The odds on a girl that ugly finding a man on the street were 100–1. Willie was that one!

Things must have gone well for the newlyweds, for I had not seen Willie in the V-D clinic for over two months. In the gym, he was well behaved and worked hard. Chris called me over and pointed to Willie.

"What's the matter with Willie. Is he sick?"

"No, he's just found the Lord," I said.

But you had to know Willie to know that he could not live with things going right. One day he came to the office looking forlorn and uncharacteristically sad.

"What's up, Willie? Things starting to go bad in the matrimonial bed?"

Willie squirmed. "Well, Doc, she is a fine girl. My house is spic-and-span clean. All my clothes is pure and clean. She even shines my gym shoes. And Doc, that girl can cook better than my grandma."

"Well, don't tell me you got bedroom problems?"

Willie smiled his shy smile. "Naw, Doc, you know I'm a perfessor of sex. She's good. I taught her good."

"Well, what, then?"

"You know she ain't pretty. We sleeps by the window. When the sun comes up, the first rays hit her face. I just lay there looking at this girl's gorilla face, snot and all sliding out her nose. Snoring loud as the Queen Mary. And her eyes all stuck together with pus. And I got to shake her and wake her up saying, 'Sing something pretty, baby. Sing!' I can't take it no more. I tried to be good, but I failed."

Willie went back to his whoring ways, and a great sigh of relief came from the girls of the Ghetto Demons. Willie was back!

Things happened in the ghetto that would be remarked upon in a normal neighborhood. One was a near-death experience.

I was getting into my car, and it was close to midnight. I was plumb exhausted. Suddenly, I faced an angry, ugly face with a .38 pistol in my face.

"Gimme yo money."

I handed him all my pocket change, which couldn't have been over twenty dollars.

He said, "All yo money or I blow your face off."

"Man, that's all I got. I'm the doctor of this clinic. I don't charge *no* money. I ain't got no more money."

The click of the revolver's hammer told me he wasn't listening to me and in the next few seconds I'd be ghetto history.

A figure suddenly appeared behind him, and then a devastating left hook caught the gunman behind his ear. He fell like a sack of wet cement. He was sprawled out in the middle of Tenth Street.

"He look peaceful for a bad guy, don't he, Doc?" asked Willie. "Let's go, leave him."

"Leave him there, in the middle of the street, knocked out? Someone may run over him," I said.

"Hope it's a Greyhound bus," said Willie, disappearing down the back alley he had come from.

In the ghetto, or in the gym, no one mentioned that story, least of all Willie. In the ghetto, you protect your own, and in that Overtown ghetto, I was the king. Untouchable.

*   *   *

"Is that far? Is there water to cross? Is it deep?"

That's the way Willie received the news from Chris Dundee that he was sending Willie to Sweden to be the sparring partner for Jimmy Ellis, the interim heavyweight champion of the world, who was scheduled to put his title on the line against Floyd Patterson.

Floyd was over the hill a bit, but he was a dangerous man for Ellis. It was such a big fight that ABC assigned Howard Cosell to do the call. We continued by having the Butch Cassidy and Sundance Kid of sparring partners: Willie and Oliver Wright. Girls of Sweden be prepared!

I, for one, was overjoyed. I loved the idea of Stockholm. We would stay at an elegant, first-rate hotel, the Forresta. The weather in September was cool but nice. The sun set around four in the afternoon. The hotel was situated next to a huge museum of a gorgeous sculpture. The sculptor was world famous.

I knew his work well, but try as I might, I couldn't remember his name. After all, I am a painter. I don't.pay too much mind to sculptors.

The main excitement for me was the presence of a film crew from England shooting Anton Chekhov's *Sea Gull*. It starred the incredibly regal and beautiful Vanessa Redgrave, who was carrying on hot and heavy with an Italian leading-man type, and also featured James Mason, Simone Signoret, Harry Andrews, and Denholm Elliot. And Kathleen Widdoes, who was doing . . . ahem . . . Willie!

When the shock of that piece of news wore off, Chickie Ferrara, the old teacher of Angelo and a top corner man, sat down next to me. "I just traded my room with you so you'd have a nice view of the bay and the town."

"Gee, thanks, Chickie." I knew there must be a catch—old New Yorkers don't give away "nuttin' for nuttin.'"

That night, as a bright half moon spread its beauty over the glittering bay, the lights of downtown Stockholm reflected on the water. I heard the first sounds, slight at first, then building in intensity. It sounded like a ten-round bout was going on next door.

I heard a female voice, clear, polished, cultured, and pleasing.

"Hit me again, Willie. Harder! Harder!"

I could hear the slaps land and then another supplication: "Make love to me, you beast," etc., etc. Use your imagination.

Next morning, at breakfast, she looked radiant. Willie and I looked frazzled. Lack of sleep will do that to you.

We were there for seven days. The nocturnal bout never let up.

"How's the view, Doc?" Chickie Ferrara would ask every morning. Everyone at the table would break out laughing.

Finally, the night of the fight arrived. Willie had to leave first, for his was an early undercard fight. He was to fight a tall Finn who couldn't fight at all and was stiff as a board. With Willie's great sense of boxing rhythm and style, it should have been a short fight. But Willie had put in fourteen nights of fighting. He was punched out.

I went to the bar to pick up my doctor's kit, which I had left in the dining room. There, sitting at the bar, shooting down straight doubles, was Kathleen. The scene was a late thirties film noir tableau. Even the bartender, drying glasses, slow, deliberate, and bored, looked like a film extra. He motioned to her with his head, as if to say, "Can you get rid of her?"

"Doc," she said, raising her beautiful tear-stained face to look at me. "I'm so worried."

"About what?" I deadpanned.

"About Willie. Will he be injured? Can he *die* out there? Will he be *hurt*?"

"Not the part you're interested in, no. That's covered by a protector." She didn't flinch but ordered another vodka double shot. I turned to leave. "He'll be back in a minute. Why don't you wait in the room?"

"I can't. My husband"—a famous TV actor—"is coming from the States any moment. I must meet him."

"Well, good luck. You'd better put more makeup on the black and blue marks on your face." The morals of people in Hollywood are very similar to the ones we have in the ghetto. I understood.

The fight played out just as it figured to. Although the giant, ultrabright, white fighter moved with slothlike speed, Willie was even slower. Once the Finn learned that Willie had no power in his punches and was virtually motionless in the middle of the ring, he teed off on Willie and administered a ten-round ass-kicking.

Willie came out half stumbling, half carried by Oliver Wright. He looked at me through puffy eyes, and through his swollen lips he said, "At least he couldn't knock me out."

"You idiot, you should have dove to the canvas."

He looked hurt. "You know I don't dive for no one."

"What happened? Couldn't you help in the corner?" I yelled at Oliver, as if, somehow, it was his fault. Outrage filled his ugly face.

"Shit, Doc, every time I yelled, 'Jab, jab,'" and here he made the hand motion of a jab, "Willie did this." He repeated the jab motion, but with his pelvis, not his hand. "Boy jus' pussied himself out," he said disgustedly.

"Kin I sleep in your room tonight, Doc?"

"No problem. Your girl's husband has come to visit for a week. Your fighting nights are over!"

"Have mercy, Lawd, have mercy," said an exhausted and beaten fighter, his eyes closing in a deep sleep, a smile on his swollen lips.

Willie was a young man when the end came suddenly. Some men live life to the fullest. They burn the candle at both ends. In his short life,

Willie lived three or four lifetimes. He missed death by inches. It never bothered him. He didn't care. He didn't even notice.

I came home from a road trip, and I saw from Ms. Mabel's expression that something was wrong.

"You can cut down on buying penicillin now," she said. It took me a minute to figure out what that meant.

"Willie?" I asked, my heart sinking.

"Yep. Last night he got to arguing with his ho and she pulled a thirty-eight and drilled him twice in the groin. Hit a major artery. Willie died on the way to the hospital."

I felt like I'd been shot in the heart.

I hated to go to the 5th Street Gym that afternoon. You would have thought that they had shot the president (again).

Chris was busy handling his calls. None concerned Willie, who was gone and forgotten. Biz as usual. Angelo, in his quiet, nice way, had made the funeral arrangements. As usual, Chris and Angelo picked up the tab.

The bell rang, and a welterweight kid from Nicaragua squared off against a lightweight from Panama. Florentino punished the heavy bag with thunderous punches. Willie Pastrano whipped the light bag with blinding speed, and the swish, swish of Luis Manuel's rope-jumping feet brought the gym back to life.

Life in the 5th Street Gym went on. Oh, yes. We were used to death in the 5th Street Gym. We just didn't pay it no mind.

"Whaddya expect. It's *boxing!*" Chris Dundee would say by way of explanation.

The Greatest Fight in Miami History

Frankie Otero

There is not one scintilla of doubt that the greatest fight in Miami history was the close fight between the British ex-champion Kenny Buchanan and the wildly popular local favorite, a dynamic, hard-punching contender named Frankie Otero. I select this because of the "package."

By "package" I mean everything that goes into making a great fight night. On the night of May 29, 1972, the Miami Convention Center was filled to capacity, standing room only, with screaming Cuban immigrants. Frankie was unquestionably the only thing that the Cuban immigrants could agree about without an argument. Frankie Otero was "their" champion. His buoyant, boyish grin, his funny personality, and his ferocity made him the most popular athlete of the whole Cuban experience.

Frankie had arrived at the high plateau of an undefeated contender. He needed one more qualifying fight to get a title shot. Frankie was ready. His public demanded it. Chris gave it to them.

Frankie Otero was a pure Miami product, born in Miami and trained at the 5th Street Gym and bred there. He developed into a champion-caliber fighter by the match-making genius of Chris Dundee, who needed a local attraction he could count on to sell out the house. Otero

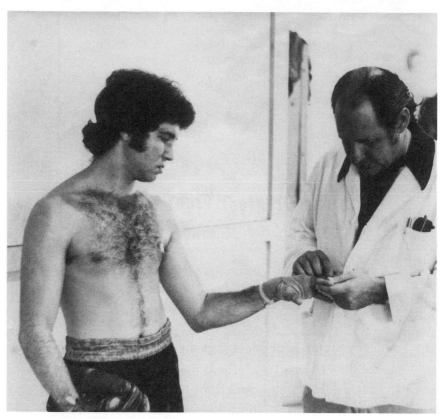

Ferdie treats Frankie Otero's hand. Lynn Pelham.

was taught how to box by Richard Riesgo. Frankie was what we call, in boxing, a protected fighter.

If you came to root for the popular lad, you were virtually assured a victory by Chris's clever match making and Frankie's underrated talents. If Frankie were to have *lost* a fight at the arena, it would have been considered a national disaster. The sellout Cuban audiences came to see Frankie Otero win, and he *never* disappointed them. Frankie always won!

The fights grew tough, and Frankie had to fight tougher and tougher opponents. But he continued to win.

Frankie had an attractive, self-denigrating joking manner about him. He didn't take himself seriously, nor did he get big headed as he won fight after fight against increasingly better opponents.

Finally, one bright day in the 5th Street Gym, after a particularly grueling fight which Frankie won by a wide margin, Chris broke the good news to Frankie.

"Frankie, great news! *Ring* magazine has rated you number one contender in the whole wide world!"

Frankie took the news quietly and said, "Chris, does this mean I have to fight *real fights* now?"

There were always half truths in what Frankie said to disparage himself. Although he was undefeated, with most of his wins earned by knockouts, Frankie wasn't ever quite sure he was a *real* fighter. But he was. Trust me, he was the real goods; it's just that *he* didn't know it.

I had worked the corners of all the Angelo Dundee fighters: Willie Pastrano, Luis Manuel Rodriguez (ninety-five fights), all of Jimmy Ellis, and seventeen years with Muhammad Ali. I had seen a lot of great fights over twenty years. The best fight of all of them, bar none, no question about it, was the "Thrilla in Manila"—Ali-Frazier III. That was the closest you could come to real life and death. If the last round

Frankie Otero a winner; Richie Riesgo raises his arm in victory. Lynn Pelham.

would have been allowed to continue, Frazier could have been killed. Such was the ugly ferocity of that fight.

But what I am writing about here is The Best Fight in Miami History. (There is an argument for Cassius Clay–Sonny Liston I, but it *wasn't* a good fight. It was a surprise, yes. It was a major upset, yes. But a good fight, no. A great audience, no. Trust me, it wasn't even close. Everyone had bet the heavy favorite, Liston, at 9 to 1.) The mood of the audience was somber. Frankie knew he was in over his head. Richard Riesgo, Luis Sarria, and I knew that Frankie faced the toughest test of his career. Even Chris, happily counting the money pouring in from a sellout crowd at the Convention Center crowd, knew it. I prayed Frankie wouldn't get humiliated by a one-way beating and a knockout in the early rounds.

As it turned out, I needn't have worried.

Frankie came to the dressing room as he always did, acting as if he didn't have a care in the world. We were all serious as hell, trying to get Frankie ready to face hell.

In the third round, Chris Dundee came up to the corner rubbing his hands. "It's a sellout, Frankie. Standing room only. They're standing in the aisles." He was bubbling over with joy.

"Chris, if we do good with the Britisher, can I have some more money?" asked Frankie with an impish grin.

"Aww, take care of the Limey, let me take care of the money," said Chris, scuttling away from ringside.

Frankie took the first two rounds as Ken, held off, was boxing splendidly but losing both rounds to Frankie, who had given all he had in his tank. Round three, came the time for Kenny to present the bill. Frankie fought back hard, but it was evident that Ken Buchanan had been a champion and he fought like a champion. Frankie survived and came back to fight a tough fourth round.

Ed Pope, editor of the *Miami Herald*, wrote, "Frankie Otero came back in the fourth with renewed vigor. He was being carried on the backs of the corner. Dr. Pacheco, Richard Riesgo and Luis Sarria gave Frankie a championship corner. All during the hard fight they gave him leadership and revived him and Frankie Otero didn't let them down."

Truer words were never written. I'd seen Angelo Dundee work miracles in the corner. I knew how to do it, and so did Riesgo and Sarria. We staggered into the tenth. The entire Convention Center crowd was on its feet. Hundreds of Cuban flags were waving. Bongo bands were playing in the corner, and a mob fresh from the rafts of the *balseros* sang a ragged but loud "Guantanamera," the song of the Cuban exiles. It was thrilling, but we had a badly beaten fighter on our hands. All three of us loved Frankie like a son. Send him out? Just to satisfy a crowd? He could be hurt, and—just maybe—he could be killed. Boxing is a serious business.

"To hell with it, he ain't gonna knock me out," said Frankie, and he staggered out to the brutal tenth. Kenny Buchanan awaited him. I caught Buchanan's eye at the beginning of round ten. He seemed to be saying, "Don't worry, Doc, I'm going easy on Frankie." I don't know today if that is what he meant. I do know that Kenny went easy in the tenth. He did not press for a knockout, which he easily could. He let Frankie go to enjoy his night. Like "Rocky," Frankie made it to ten. He had won his personal battle. To this day, I give thanks to Kenny every time I see him at fights I call in London. Kenny Buchanan was a champion that night. And so was Frankie Otero.

Frankie fought on for a few more years, but he never again reached the heights of greatness that he did that cool May night in the Convention Center. If you only get one such night in your life, consider yourself lucky. It's enough.

Fortunately, Frankie lived a great family life with a beautiful wife and a successful son. He remains young in looks and has the same infectious sense of humor. He still denigrates his value as a fighter.

But all of us who had the pleasure of seeing Frankie fight all of his fights knew that Frankie was a major top-ranked fighter. That night, he was a champion.

21

My Memories of Dr. Ferdie Pacheco

Budd Schulberg

Over the course of my long life, I've had the pleasure of meeting a number of interesting and talented people, but there is only one that I would qualify as a "Renaissance man." He is Dr. Ferdie Pacheco, popularly known as "the fight doctor" because of his long association with Muhammad Ali, going all the way back to the Miami days when "the greatest" was still Cassius Clay, trained by Pacheco's ebullient buddy Angelo Dundee, in the gritty 5th Street Gym. Ali was a fistic Roman candle, and the patient, resilient, and accomplished physician was the ideal medical guide for him. Typical of Dr. Ferdie's social sense was his setting up two practices in Miami: one for the prosperous or economically comfortable, the other in the ghetto where patients could not afford his services unless he worked gratis, which of course he did.

Aside from his busy professional schedule, the "fight doctor" also found time to paint (his work commanding five-figure prices), became an impressive cartoonist, and wrote impressive books about his roots in Ybor City, the colorful Cuba-cultured city-within-a-city in Tampa, while conducting a handful of careers, including promoting fights for NBC and becoming a much sought-after public speaker. I'm sure I am leaving something out, as it's not easy to keep up with a man who has so many strings to his bow that he really needs a harp.

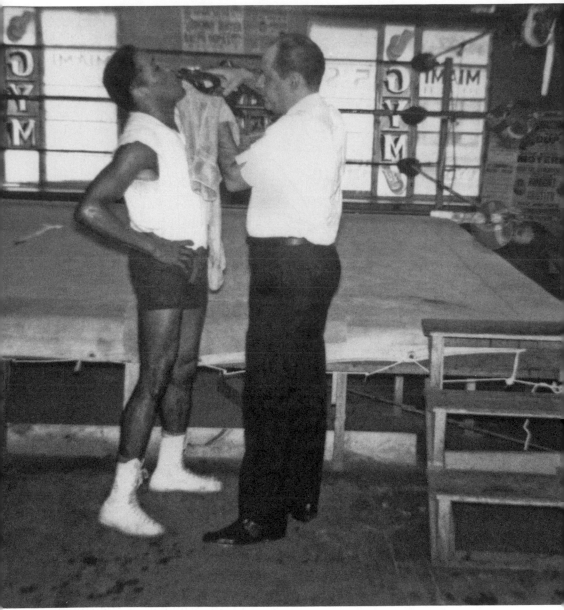

Ferdie giving water to Luis Manuel Rodriguez. Kurt Severin.

Whenever the fight doctor calls me, I feel the magnetic energy, the range of his interests, his enthusiasm for life—yes, he's talkative but it's only because he has so much to say. You listen and you learn and you thank the god of friendship that has drawn you into the inner circle of this unique contributor to boxing's mystique.

On Budd Schulberg

Ferdie Pacheco

One of the main reasons I feel so indebted to boxing and my days in the 5th Street Gym is the wonderful friendship I developed with Budd Schulberg. Aside from the Dundees and Ali, Schulberg is the single most important development. His friendship has been vital and important to my career as a writer. His keen understanding of the science of boxing helped me in my call of a fight. His sense of history infuses all that he does when watching boxing today. And last, and most important of all, he brings class and a sense of history to boxing.

All during my long college career, I was aware of Budd's writing ability. Together we took apart and studied three crucial novels. They were the same: a fearless writer got inside and behind the scene to write an exposé, first in big-time boxing, second in the rotten world of Hollywood, and, finally, in the crooked world of union dominance of the Jersey waterfront. All three were gems of writing. The characters were so true. There wasn't a false note in all three stories. Never in my life did I think I would have the luck to just meet Budd, much less become his friend.

Because I lucked out and found the door into big-time boxing when I became the doctor for the 5th Street Gym, I found myself being introduced to the famous Budd Schulberg. He stood quietly at ringside watching Ali spar. With him was his gorgeous redheaded wife, Geraldine Brooks, an award-winning actress. Both were mesmerized by Ali.

Chris always went out of his way to make the famous pair comfortable. He took me aside and growled, "That guy is a famous writer; he did *The Harder They Fall*."

"My favorite film in boxing. That's Budd Schulberg. I'll take him over. Don't worry."

"Don't give any tickets away free."

As if I *had* any tickets to give away. Chris always said, "You give one sucker a free ticket, and forget about him ever buying a ticket again."

Budd at sixty was a ruggedly handsome man. A broken nose and massive shoulders made him look like a tough guy. But he wasn't. He was a surprising pussycat. He was thrilled as I suggested that we would take him *inside* Ali's dressing room. Shyly, he asked if his wife could come in also. Ali never permitted women in his dressing room, but I knew how to get around that. After all, Ali was, if nothing else, a rabid ladies man, and Geraldine was gorgeous. Later on, at the height of our friendship, I would save her life, in what I consider the only genuine miracle I was ever involved with. But that still lay ahead.

"Ali, Budd is the best writer in boxing, and he wrote *The Harder They Fall*, the best boxing movie ever made."

"With Humphrey Bogart? And Max Baer and Slapsie Maxie. And a lot of old guys. Two-ton Tony Galento? Yeah, I saw that. Was any of that true?" His eyes were open wide. He was hooked. Ali was a dyed-in-the-wool movie fan.

"One hundred percent true," I said and deferred to Budd.

"Boxing was very crooked in those days because the mob had control of it. So, they called the shots," Budd said by way of explanation.

"Didn't they bother you about writing about them?"

"No. They were scared of me," said Budd, stuttering badly. Budd has a wicked sense of humor.

Ali shot me a look and saw that I was laughing, so he dug the fact that Budd was putting him on. He slapped Budd on the back, and from that moment to the present Ali has remembered him that way. "That's the guy who backed down the Mafia, and he wrote the truth."

After an enjoyable fifteen minutes in the presence of Ali, as an exclusive interview, I took them down to our lunch place, Puerto de Sagua. There Angelo, Chris, Sarria, and a couple of the gray men greeted Budd with the reverence he deserved. Boxing people love *The Harder They Fall*. The old guys were full of old-time stories. After all, these were their days. They knew all about Primo Cernera and Frankie Carbo and Blinky Palermo. Chris was beaming. The boys took in Budd. He was welcomed into the inner family of the 5th Street Gym. After all, he had exposed the Mafia and lived to tell about it.

Once Budd was in my clutches, I was determined not to let him go. He was mine. I took him to my lovely home and dazzled him with a houseful of my oil paintings. He and Geraldine loved them. He marveled at my ten-thousand-book library. He was a book junkie like me.

He spent his week at the 5th Street Gym. The boxers soon became aware of who the attractive couple from Hollywood was, and they clustered around, getting autographs like stricken teenagers. The Schulbergs were the main attraction of the week. I could see that Budd ate it up. He was "inside" the Ali Circus and accepted as a member of the 5th Street Gym family.

I had an inspiration. I gave him supper that night and at the end of a very successful night, at the appropriate moment, casually asked, "Budd, why don't Geraldine and you join us? I'll make the travel arrangements and hotel reservations. You can't really appreciate Ali until

Left to right: Budd Schulberg, Ferdie, and Angelo Dundee. Luisita Sevilla Pacheco.

you spend a week before the fight with him. The fight is nothing, and I'll get you into the corner. You'll see the championship corner in action."

I thought that he was going to hug and kiss me. "So, you want to go?" I said jestingly. And thus started a memorable partnership, which lasted until Ali finally hung up his gloves, unfortunately way too late. Budd was there in the front-row seat.

Right here, as I write about this wonderful friendship, I must express a surprising disappointment.

Schulberg was "inside" the corner in all fights. He was particularly active in the Rumble in the Jungle and then the best heavyweight championship fight in history—the Thrilla in Manila, Ali versus Frazier, which was life and death from round ten on. Budd Schulberg was there, right in the corner.

And yet, and yet, Budd never produced the masterpiece I thought he would do. Perhaps he had gone too far past that point where you lose objectivity, you get too close. The hounds of the journalist put out one

Left to right: Luis Sarria, Budd Schulberg, and Ferdie at the 5th Street Gym. Kurt Severin.

sloppy book after another about Ali. Norman Mailer even managed to get inside the corner, and to hear him tell it, he got into Ali's brain and could quote what Ali was thinking. What rubbish!

The fights cried out for a clear-thinking boxing expert to analyze what was happening, to bring all that he knew about Ali and his corner without prejudice, and combine that with his sharp analysis of how the fight evolved. Budd Schulberg should have written the definitive story of those two fights. He didn't. He died on August 5, 2009. I was sorry he didn't live to see this book, which has so much of him in it

22

Death in the Ring

The 5th Street Gym was a classroom for boxers, for their lives in and out of the ring. Of all the topics that were never discussed, the main one was the possibility of dying in the ring. Death was never brought up—not by the promoters, including Chris Dundee; not by the many trainers, from Angelo Dundee on down; not by the old gray men who worked the corners.

On proper retrospect, one has to ask why they *should* bring up that ghastly subject, for it would put a fear of boxing in the boxer's mind. Well, when is the appropriate time to discuss death?

Never.

Boxing deaths just happen, like an iceberg that suddenly looms up before a ship. You can't avoid it. It hits you, and you live or you die. Then it and you disappear, until the next time.

When I went to the gym, I tried to bring up the subject of fatality after each death, and I was always met by a sea of blank faces. "Yeah, shit happens. It's too bad." And they would turn back to their solitary task of training.

I worked in the corners with twelve champions. I spent twenty-five years in corners. But after each fight, I reverted to being a doctor, so my experience is solitary.

The champions I saw fight past "Stop!" who paid for it with brain damage included Willie Pastrano, deceased in his fifties; Ralph Dupas;

Luis Manuel Rodriguez, deceased in his fifties; Jimmy Ellis, who suffered blindness and nerve damage; Muhammad Ali, with Parkinson's; and Jerry Quarry, deceased. I have to add Joe Frazier, who took three colossal beatings at the hands of Ali, and too many lesser boxers to mention.

The old Cuban trainer Luis Sarria was indispensable. He was an encyclopedia of boxing knowledge. I stuck to him like glue in the gym. In particular, he was great at spotting when the boxer was starting the downhill slide.

Sarria looked at these elements:

1. The jab. Was it losing its snap? Did he *pop* a jab and move away (Ali, Pastrano), or as the boxer faded did the jab become slow and lazy? Did he have trouble getting back to block the counter? We had one of the finest jabbers in the business in Luis Manuel Rodriguez. He had 110 fights and won over 95 percent of them. But he always had to fight bigger men with heavier punches. I felt that he was through one night in San Francisco, when he was fighting a Mexican guy whom he had knocked out six months before. The first round started, and Sarria and I looked at each other. "That's it. He is shot!" I yelled, and Sarria agreed. Luis Manuel was not only *not* landing his jab, but he was getting gonged by a countering right hand repeatedly. Luis Manuel, for the first time, was stopped by a ham-and-egger. The remaining course of his life was downhill, ending in a sad, messy collapse at age fifty.

2. The legs. Great defensive fighters have great wheels. Ali, Pastrano, and Luis Manuel were virtual ballerinas. Men with tree-trunk legs like Foreman, Liston, and Frazier withstood heavy punches. But when the legs quit, the body and head are in for a savage beating. If the legs go, and that is easily visible, the fighter must retire. To stay is an open invitation to brain damage. Unfortunately, they don't recognize it or are in denial, and hence, after age thirty-five (on average), they should go. They don't.

3. Speech. Put all of Ali's press conferences on a long tape and review the course and history of Ali's brain damage. At first, he is greased lightning, talking a million miles a minute. At the end, he is mumbling, stumbling. It's hard to watch, but he wouldn't heed the warnings.

4. Ideation. Chris Dundee, the hardened old pro promoter, had a phrase to cover boxers who do bizarre things after they retire. No matter what the crime, Chris would say, "Whaddaya expect? The man was a fighter." That covered any explanation needed. Chris was right: "Whaddaya expect?"

5. Ability to take a punch. Whereas the prior fights had shown a rock-hard jaw, suddenly, one night, he can't take even a stiff jab. Luis Manuel Rodriguez got knocked out by a jab—impossible, but there it was. You reach one night when you have to tell your fighter, "That's it for tonight, kid, it ain't your night." Left unspoken is that it will never be his night again.

To explain why a fighter continues in spite of all that evidence of future damage, in spite of the beatings and the prospective loss of self-esteem in a fighter who knows nothing else and wants to go on, money (or the lack of it) is a prime consideration. The explanations are many, but in the end, somebody should be around to stop the fighter. Such is the nature of boxing, though that will never happen.

We are stuck with a punch-drunk syndrome. While I was the head of NBC boxing, I tried to stop fighters from coming back. I had it done. Then George Foreman and Sugar Ray Leonard decided to come back. Everything I had accomplished exploded in my face.

And that allowed Julio Cesar Chavez, Roberto Duran, and Foreman to return to fight at over fifty years of age. A disgrace? Yes, but you pay to see them fight. We're all guilty.

The old guys are still tottering into the ring to sustain irreparable and irreversible brain damage, most of which is incurred after that night that tells you, "This ain't your night, kid!"

One of the many things I saw in the boxing ring that I could not condone or find an excuse for, or that did not fit into my code of life, was

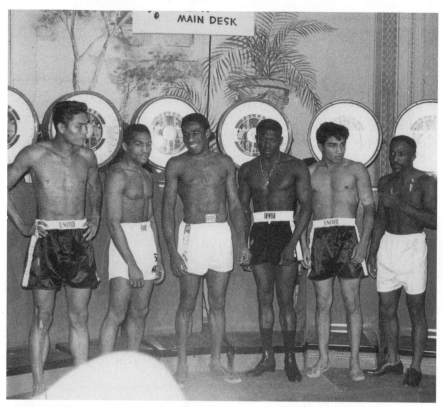

The weigh-in for the 1963 championship fight in Dodger Stadium, Los Angeles. *Left to right*: Roberto de la Cruz, Ultiminio "Sugar" Ramos, Luis Manuel Rodriguez, Emile Griffith, Battling Torres, Davey Moore. Enrique Encinosa Collection.

the death of a boxer. Every time I was a witness to or part of a boxing death, I came home to sleepless nights. Why was I, an ethical physician with a large charity practice, part of a sport that allowed death? Why was I part of the corner work which encouraged, exhorted, and sent one man to hurt the other to the point at which death results? I never found a suitable answer. I don't have one now. I don't know if there is one. I suppose I have to say that it's a character flaw. My first death in the ring occurred when Ultiminio Ramos ended the life of the "Springfield Rifle," Davey Moore. Those were the days of three-strand ropes. Had there been four strands, Davey's head would have been caught and he would not have been slammed into the hard canvas floor. That certainly was one thing to fix. I did. When I became head of the NBC boxing department, I campaigned hard to put in the fourth rope, and today we have the fourth rope.

As I have discussed elsewhere in the book, I believe the main reason for death is a big beating during the fight *before* the one in which the death occurred. This is entirely avoidable. Good record keeping with computerized records that are instantly available and a boxing commission with balls would prevent those deaths. In the avoidable Emile Griffith versus Benny Paret tragedy, a cursory review of Paret's record would have revealed that Paret took a monstrous beating at the hands of Gene Fullmer, a middleweight with a heavy punch, in his previous bout. Paret's brain was softened up, and it blew up on him.

Benny "Kid" Paret. Enrique Encinosa Collection.

Alejandro Lavarante took a big beating from Ali; then, in his next bout, he died. Why did they make the fight? Who allowed it?

Cleveland Denny was a better-than-average kid who went to Montreal to fight a very tough local favorite, Gaeton Hart. There had been bad blood between them. Again, Cleveland came off a tough fight. I was in Montreal to do the first Leonard-Duran fight for an independent Pay Per View company. Cleveland Denny was taking a savage beating by Gaeton Hart. By the fifth round, it was obviously over, but the referee and the corners were brave and the hometown crowd wanted it to go on, so the one-way beating continued. I was yelling at the boxing commissioners to step in and stop it, but they wouldn't. Suddenly Cleveland Denny slumped in the corner, but Hart continued to beat him with a vicious two-handed attack. Cleveland finally pitched forward onto his face.

I was livid as I watched helplessly at my broadcast position, but then I saw that the corner men were having trouble opening Cleveland's mouth to extract his mouthpiece. They didn't know why Cleveland's jaws were clenched. I did. Blood was hemorrhaging down between the two hemispheres of the brain, interfering with the muscles' inhibitory nerves. As they short-circuited, the muscles went into spasms. Minutes were precious, as there was very little time. Where was the doctor? Not present. Where were the paramedics? None. Where was the ambulance? None. Anybody? No one was there as Cleveland was dying. Someone finally woke up and called an ambulance. Almost an hour later, he was in surgery. Too late. Cleveland Denny lingered for a few days more in the hospital, a living vegetable, and then he died.

Could he have been saved by immediate attention? Possibly. Certainly, with the hour-long wait, he had no chance at all.

Not to have a physician at ringside was criminal.

And where, do you imagine, was that ring physician? In the upper deck, looking for a hot dog to eat! Criminal dereliction of duty!

I ripped off my headset and told my broadcast partner, an old pro named Bill Mauser, to keep talking, and I went into the ring to help.

When I got back to NBC, I went straight to Don Ohlmeyer and told him of the horrifying night and asked permission to use NBC to attack boxing's cavalier attitude toward death in the ring. First of all, I suggested that no boxing match would take place on NBC shows without a contract for an ambulance in place at ringside. No ambulance, no fight. I can't tell you how gutsy a call that was for Ohlmeyer and President Arthur Watson. By the time the flak about the cost was over, we had won, and today there are ambulances at all events because of NBC. That worked out well, and Ohlmeyer gave me the go-ahead. I began a campaign for boxing safety that lasted for the ten years that I was at NBC. We led the fight, I'm proud to say, and changed a great many faults, which in turn had an impact on diminishing boxing deaths.

One of the biggest corrections was the change in the attitude of referees and corner men when it came to stopping a fight. Historically, the promoter and the crowd wanted to see a match to the finish. Stopping a fight prematurely was considered to be the end of a boxer's career. No one wanted a merciful referee. Merciful officials never worked another fight!

I came blasting into the picture with a microphone and direct scathing criticism of insanely brave referees. But no longer would we refuse to identify him by name. Now, every guilty referee, corner man, or manager got called by name. Mistakes were magnified by slow-motion replays. With clever evidence of mistakes and of reluctance to stop the beating, with their names clearly on national television, they started to change.

Before a fight, at the weigh-in they would sidle up to me and quietly plead, "Please don't call my name. My family is catching hell because of what you're saying about me."

"Well, my boy, just do your job. Don't fuck up. Don't cause a death, and you'll not hear your name except in praise when you do your job right."

Slowly, boxing became more humane. For that permission to ruthlessly attack the guilty, I give my public thanks to Don Ohlmeyer, executive producer, and to the late Arthur Watson, president of NBC. They let me preach and teach about blindness in boxing because of detached retinas. We even had an age restriction until George Foreman came along with his early easy fights. They banned female boxing (ugh).

We had many small victories with the commissions and with boxing managers, trainers, and referees. I was proud of the work we did and the record we left.

I sort of put a huge Band-Aid on my conscience for the sins I committed when I worked in the corners. I think there are fewer deaths now and fewer fearsome beatings. Also, regrettably, there are fewer loudmouthed announcers willing to identify and criticize incompetent officials and bad rules. And as with everything in boxing, old habits slide back in. Money talks. Old washed-up fighters keep fighting, plodding on doggedly, suffering defeat after defeat, sliding into neurological damage or the punch-drunk syndrome, Parkinson's disease, Alzheimer's, and eventually death. Why? Because the "public wants to see it." That translates to money and ratings. As one old gray man of the 5th Street Gym said to me, "Only the fighters die."

The End of Chris Dundee

Suzanne Dundee Bonner

As the daughter of Chris Dundee and a capable aide to her father, Suzanne Dundee Bonner contributed the finest chapter, by far, in this book. This elegant, heartfelt look at her relation to her deceased father is a classic.

"Higher, Daddy, higher!" The little two-year-old shrieked with delight. The man picked her up in his arms and tossed her in the air. They were in the parking lot of the old Yankee Stadium. The man gently put her down, took her hand, and began to quickly walk to the entrance. The little girl had to run to keep up with his pace.

"Where do you want to go first?" he asked. "Want to get your hot dog?"

"No, silly papoose, let's go to the press box," Sue answered, smiling.

*   *   *

It was still daylight outside. The asphalt in the parking lot felt as if it was burning right through my shoes. I could no longer hear the crowd in the stadium, and the old green building stood like an oasis in the ninety-degree heat. I entered the doors and inhaled the cool hospital air. It was hushed and dark inside with little evidence of typical hospital hustle. It was the hospital wing of a nursing home: a sobering distinction.

Suzanne with her father, Chris Dundee. Alexander Bonner.

As I approached the nursing station, I cleared my throat. "Hi. Could you tell me where my father's room is?"

The male nurse went to a central location hub to pull a chart for reference. "It's 106 . . . down the hall on your left," he said.

I took another couple of deep breaths and headed down the dark corridor. The door to the room was slightly ajar, and I noticed that the name tag by the side of the door was blank.

I stood outside the door, knowing that I would have to say good-bye to the one person I never believed would leave me. I heard footsteps and turned to see the male nurse. "Mrs. Bonner, this is 106. Are you OK? Can I help?" he asked.

"No, no, I'm his daughter," I said.

He didn't read the significance of that, but he was familiar with the ritual and he reached out and touched my arm. "He's been waiting for you." My legs were beginning to tremble, and I nodded to him, then leaned on the door and walked in.

He was lying there, very still, staring up at the ceiling. The bed rails were up. "Please, can we lower the railings?" I asked. The nurse ran toward the bed and quickly lowered the side rail. I nodded and asked for us to be left alone. I crawled up on the side of the bed and saw that he looked so fragile now. I took both of his hands. They were large, strong hands. "Dad," I whispered, "I'm here now." He continued looking up at the ceiling as if he were viewing the entire galaxy. I swallowed hard and fought back the tears. I wouldn't cry; I was too much like him. My father's eyes closed, and he turned his head toward me. He squeezed my hands tightly and opened his eyes. I knew that this was the right moment, so I told him what I believed he was waiting to hear. "Dad, it's OK, you can let go now." I choked on the words. He continued looking at me with his intense eyes, the eyes of the wizard. We held hands for an eternity. Then he seemed to have had enough, and his eyes went back to that spot on the ceiling. I knew that it was time to make the calls to the family.

I went back down the hall to the nurses' station and told them that I needed to use the phone. They hustled about and showed me to a private room. I called my husband first, then my dad's brother, and then his son, my brother. I needed to tell them that it was time to come say good-bye.

I waited for my uncle, and shortly I saw him coming down the hall. He put his arms around me, and then he stood back and touched my cheek. His hands looked like my father's hands: big, strong, gentle. I led him toward the room. "I'll go in with you, if you want," I whispered. "I think that he can hear you."

My uncle had a sick smile on his face. "Sue, I can't do this alone. Please, you'd better come in with me," he said.

He stood at my father's bedside talking to him in a soft, low voice that I could not hear, and he kept looking over to me for encouragement. He whispered, "Honey, he's looking up at the ceiling. What is he looking at?"

"The stars," I answered. I thought back to what the fighter said to him when they were making the film: "Look at me, godfather; I'm a 'moving star.'" I walked my uncle to the door and kissed him good-night. Then I went inside the room to wait. I sat on the side of my father's bed and wrapped my arms around him, knowing that I could not hold him there, that I was powerless—the wizard was powerless.

He would no longer look at me, and I realized that he wanted to make this journey alone. I lightly pressed my lips on his mouth and whispered, "Good-bye, my sweet papoose."

It was a few minutes after 11 p.m., and we were lying in bed with the lights off. My husband had come home from seeing my father an hour earlier. He told me that Dad didn't really seem to see or hear him. He said that he was staring up at the ceiling. I smiled. I knew that I was the only one the wizard could see, just me and maybe the "moving star."

The loud ringing brought me back around, and I quickly picked up the phone. I looked at the clock. "Mrs. Bonner," the voice said. "This is Douglas Gardens." Then there was silence on the other end. I sat up in bed. "Yes, I've been waiting for your call," I answered.

Chris Dundee passed away November 16, 1998, at 11 p.m.

Index

Page numbers in *italics* indicate illustrations.

Ferdie Pacheco, M.D., has been called a Renaissance man because of his multifaceted career. He has been successful as a pharmacist, a medical doctor, a fight doctor, and as a corner man for twelve world champions, including Muhammad Ali, for seventeen years. He also served as a boxing commentator for NBC, Showtime, and Univision, winning two Emmys, and was the boxing consultant for NBC for ten years.

Dr. Pacheco saw operations and autopsies as a child and at the same time started to paint. He helped finance his medical education by contributing his cartoons to major national magazines. Today he is a world-recognized fine painter and has recently focused on Florida history, specializing in Ybor City, where he was born of Spanish parents. He has been exhibiting his work in galleries since 1983. The awards for his art include Gold Medal and First Prize in Tonneins, France, and Best Colorist at the Musée du Luxembourg in Paris. His paintings are in the collections of many leading personalities in the world, such as Andy Garcia, Shirley MacLaine, Budd Schulberg, Petula Clark, Evander Holyfield, Lou Duva, and Ernest Borgnine, to name a few. The United Nations chose his portrait of Gandhi to be made into a U.N. postage stamp for the International Day of Nonviolence in October 2009.

As a screenwriter, he sold six scripts to major studios including Warner, Alan Ladd, King Hitzig, Paul Mazlansky, Canon Productions, and Salvatore Alabiso Productions. He appeared as an actor, playing himself, in the movie *The Great White Hype*. A movie he wrote for an Italian company, Pico Productions, called *Virtually Yours* has been distributed throughout Europe. A documentary on his life—*Ferdie Pacheco: The World of the Fight Doctor*—was shown in film festivals.

He also has had fourteen books published and has written articles, columns, and reviews for Florida magazines and newspapers. Some of his unpublished novels are currently being considered for publication. In bookstores now is *Nino Pernetti's Caffe Abbracci Cookbook*—his life story—and travels around the world.

Ferdie Pacheco has been happily married for thirty-nine years to Luisita Sevilla, noted flamenco artist and photographer, who also manages his art and types and edits his manuscripts. They live in Miami.

Luisita Sevilla Pacheco (aka Karen Louise Maestas) was born in Denver, Colorado, of American Indian and Spanish parents. She was educated in Seville, Spain, in the art of Spanish dance. For twelve years, she travelled around the world—through South America, Asia, Malaysia, Australia, New Zealand, Japan—living out of a suitcase, doing what she loved.

During her travels to Miami, she met Dr. Ferdie Pacheco through a mutual friend. They fell in love and married. Luisita opened a dance studio and taught what she loved.

Also during this time she went on trips with Ferdie to championship bouts, and as an experienced photographer she took photographs of the fights and the gyms, many of which have been exhibited in galleries and published in several books. In the past two decades, Luisita has edited many books and chosen the photographs for each one, including seven of Ferdie's books. She also wrote and provided photographs for *A Tribute to a Flamenco Dancer,* about the dance and the life of Bobby Lorca, her dance partner; she gave the profits of the book to AIDS research because he died of that disease.

She lives and works with her husband in Miami managing his art. They have a daughter, Tina, who is a film editor.

Other Books by Ferdie Pacheco

Title	Publisher	Year
Fight Doctor	Simon and Schuster	1976, 1977
Fight Doctor	Stanley Paul, London	1976, 1978, 1979
Muhammad Ali: A View from the Corner	Carol Publishing	1992
Renegade Lightning	Presidio Press	1992
Ybor City Chronicles	University Press of Florida	1994, 2004
Columbia Restaurant Cook Book	University Press of Florida	1995, 2004
Pacheco's Art of Ybor City	University Press of Florida	1997, 2004
Christmas Eve Cookbook	University Press of Florida	1998, 2004
Pacheco's Art of Cubans in Exile	Avanti Press	2000
The 12 Greatest Rounds of Boxing	Total Sports Publishing	2000
Trolley Kat	Hillsborough Press	2001
Trolley Kat ABC	Hillsborough Press	2001
The 12 Greatest Rounds of Boxing	Sports Media Publishing Canada	2003
Blood in My Coffee	Sports Publications	2004
Nino Pernetti's Caffe Abbracci Cookbook	University Press of Florida	2007